REIMAGINING DETROIT

REIMAGINING DETROIT

Opportunities for Redefining an American City

John Gallagher

Detroit, Michigan

17 16 15 14 13   10 9 8 7 6

Library of Congress Cataloging-in-Publication Data

Gallagher, John, 1949–
Reimagining Detroit : opportunities for redefining an American city / John Gallagher.
          p. cm. — (A Painted Turtle book)
Includes bibliographical references and index.
ISBN 978-0-8143-3469-0 (pbk. : alk. paper)
1. Urban renewal—Michigan—Detroit. I. Title.
HT177.D4G35 2010
307.3'4160977434—dc22
2010016181

∞

Designed by Brad Norr Design
Typeset by Maya Rhodes
Composed in Bell Centennial and Serifa

This book is for Sheu-Jane

Barn's burnt down—
now
I can see the moon.

—Masahide

Contents

FOREWORD

Cities such as Detroit, Michigan; Youngstown or Cleveland, Ohio; and Muncie, Indiana, once were the backbone that sustained the middle class and helped make America one of the most prosperous nations the world has ever known. In recent decades, though, these cities have fallen on hard times. Economic and social factors have drained many of these cities of residents and businesses.

It is an undeniable fact that these cities are different than they once were and that they will be required to evolve. Fortunately, cities such as Youngstown, Pittsburgh, Cleveland, and even Detroit are beginning to recognize that being smaller doesn't have to mean being inferior. These cities are using their rich legacies to help propel them into a more viable future instead of remaining anchored to the difficulties of the past.

Aristotle held that a great city is not necessarily a populous one. Smaller cities—unlike their larger counterparts—are tailor-made for the kind of flexible innovation required to compete in the new global economy. Bureaucracies are leaner. Results can be seen more quickly. Novel approaches to public- and private-sector challenges can be kick-started on a manageable scale.

John Gallagher presents a compelling case about a viable future for these cities. The audience for his book is as wide and diverse as the people who comprise our nation's indispensable civic centers. Whether urban or rural dweller, academic or practitioner, the reader takes from Gallagher a deeper appreciation of both the challenges and opportunities that exist within our cities, challenges and opportunities that will ultimately impact our country. For, as President John F. Kennedy admonished us, "We will neglect our cities to our peril, for when we neglect them we neglect the nation."

Jay Williams, Mayor of Youngstown, Ohio

INTRODUCTION

Of the countless books written about Detroit, many chronicle the city's colorful rise: Cadillac and Chief Pontiac and Judge Woodward, Henry Ford and the Model T, Walter Reuther and the American labor movement, the Arsenal of Democracy and Motown music. Many other books dissect Detroit's fall from grace—that half-century (and counting) of riots and redlining, white flight and suburban sprawl, shuttered factories, broken dreams, and wasted lives.

In *Reimagining Detroit* I choose neither to question nor to quibble about how Detroit got where it is today. In these pages, I'll seek to answer a more pressing question: *Where do we go from here?* This book, in other words, looks only to Detroit's future, and, by extension, to the future of cities everywhere. For while Detroit may be the nation's poster city for urban dystopia, it shares its predicament to a greater or lesser degree with dozens of other cities. Population loss and industrial collapse scar cities around the globe, not just a handful of towns surrounding the Great Lakes. During this search for solutions, we'll be stopping in cities close to home, such as Flint and Cleveland and Youngstown, and others more distant, too, including Seoul and London and Dresden and Turin. All these cities offer lessons from which Detroit can learn, and Detroit can offer a few lessons to those cities, too.

The most surprising conclusion in this book about Detroit's future is that Detroit *has* a future, although not the one most people living fifty years ago expected. Even today, many politicos, like leaders around the world, tout a fantasy version of the city's comeback—repopulating the city's vast empty spaces, returning downtown to the shopping mecca it once was, and so forth. That ship sailed a long time ago. The more time and money we waste on such fantastic visions, the worse Detroit (and, again, other cities) will become. A better future awaits Detroit if those of us who call the city home make the right choices.

Perhaps the odds are long that we'll make those choices. If Detroit were more easily reformed, we might have short-circuited its slide to urban ruin earlier. Instead, the city suffers a level of dysfunction crippling in its intensity. When people say Detroit is dying, there's no reason to deny it. By any reasonable measure, from the statistics on crime and poverty to the grim aspect that the city affords to residents and visitors alike, Detroit *is* dying. But it has a chance—slim, perhaps, yet within our grasp—to live. This book is about that chance.

And where does that possibility lie? Mostly in an unqualified acceptance of Detroit as a smaller but potentially better city. This will be harder to achieve than we may think. Detroit most likely will continue to lose population for a time, and too many critics will see that loss as a death sentence. They believe that a shrinking city is a shameful place, a city getting worse. For these critics, population remains the all-important measure of victory: If it's going up, we win. If it's going down, we despair. This book challenges that misguided belief on every page. Let's start by acknowledging that when we shun the idea of a smaller city, we hinder our ability to capitalize on the advantages of being smaller. Indeed, generations have fought against urban population loss in every way imaginable—with tax abatements, federal grants, renaissance zones, big showcase projects such as stadiums and casinos, alphabet agencies such as DDAs and TIFs, and a whole lot more. These efforts nudged the needle, but in terms of reversing the long-term population loss, they have failed unambiguously in city after city. One could argue that without such heroic efforts, things would be even worse. Or one could admit that it's time to try something new.

With acceptance comes the ability to see cities in entirely new ways. Many world-class cities are smaller than Detroit in terms of population—Seattle and San Francisco and Savannah in our own country, and Vancouver and Venice in other lands. To trade Detroit's reputation as a Rust Belt failure for the allure of one of those other cities wouldn't be such a bad trade. First, though, Detroit will have to embrace getting smaller as an opportunity, not a curse. That vacant lot that we were holding for some hoped-for development? Now maybe we can turn it into a community garden to help feed the neighborhood. That eight- or ten-lane thoroughfare that no longer carries the volume of traffic for which it was designed? Now we can put it on a road diet, reducing automotive lanes by creating bicycle lanes, widening sidewalks, and running a transit line up the middle. The streams and wetlands buried generations ago to provide sewers for a growing city? Now we can rediscover these natural treasures, restoring the ecology to create a greener environment that's cooler in summer and healthier year-round. With the auto industry's collapse, we can foster a more entrepreneurial economy, nimble rather than sluggish. With city government broken, we can create new models of local leadership.

All these things become possible when a city gets smaller. Change, even change we at first perceive to be negative, brings opportunity. The challenge is to see beyond the heartache and grasp the opportunity. As Japanese poet Masahide puts it: *Barn's burnt down—now I can see the moon.*

Shrinking Cities

People who live in Detroit and Buffalo and Youngstown share a common understanding of what it means to inhabit a shrinking city. They've come to define shrinkage as a post–World War II problem centered on the Great Lakes industrial region. In that time and place, they have seen once-great cities depopulated rapidly as auto factories and steel mills shut down and new bedroom communities lured away residents. From their perspective, shrinkage stems from a witch's brew of American industrial decline, white flight, and suburban sprawl.

But in fact such an image, so familiar to an American audience, shows us only one face of city shrinkage. Cities far from the American heartland are also losing people, and for all sorts of reasons. Globalization and economic decline play a part, but so do war, famine, natural disaster, political upheaval, low birth rates, and many other events and trends.

Even in the United States, shrinkage is not just a Rust Belt phenomenon. New Orleans lost about half its population after Hurricane Katrina. San Jose, capital of Silicon Valley, saw an out-migration after the tech bubble burst in 1999 (considerably easing traffic jams, by the way. Who says there are no benefits to shrinkage?). Even the area around Orlando, in Central Florida, an area that for decades bloomed like a hothouse flower, lost 9,700 residents in the twelve months between April 2008 and April 2009. Demographers blamed the loss on the disappearance of jobs during the recession. Orange County Mayor Rich Crotty told the *Orlando Sentinel*, "We've gone from feast to famine in a pretty fast time, and these population numbers are a symptom of that. In the future, it's how do we adapt to declining growth?"[1]

Europeans show a better intuitive grasp of the complex nature of shrinkage than Americans. From the collapse of the Roman Empire to the effects of plagues and famines, over many centuries Europeans have come to understand that cities lose population now and then as part of a cycle of growing and shrinking. Today, shrinkage is a phenomenon found in both urban and rural Germany, Italy, Finland, Sweden, Spain, Hungary, and Latvia, among other nations. In the former East Germany, out-migration to the more prosperous former West Germany followed the fall of Communism. Then, too, Germany and Italy are touched by low birth rates. Causes of shrinkage overlap in many places. Some German cities saw out-migration to more economically advantaged regions at the same time they were experiencing low birth rates.[2]

Dresden, located in the southern part of the former East Germany, is a good example of the complex nature of shrinkage.[3] Buoyed by optimism after the fall of Communism in 1989 and 1990, Dresden was developing as part of the emerging microelectronics industry in what became known as the "Silicon Saxony." The city embarked on an ambitious building program, creating new retail, hospitality, and housing construction. But the population of Dresden did not keep pace. Suburbanization, out-migration to the former West Germany, and other trends saw Dresden's population slide from around 525,000 in 1990 to about 475,000 just ten years later.

Dresden's civic leaders at first ignored this trend, planning for greater growth, and then reversed course and began to plan for a shrinking city. Surprisingly, the opposite happened. The state of Saxony allowed Dresden to do what Sunbelt cities in the United States were doing at the same time—annexing nearby suburbs—so that Dresden's population began to rebound around 2000. By mid-decade the population had reached close to 500,000. That was still well below the city's pre–World War II peak of 650,000 in the 1930s. But Dresden's experience shows that shrinkage is by no means a simple, one-way story of urban decline in America's industrial Midwest.

The ebb and flow of population over time has given Europeans a more relaxed view of shrinkage. In America, with its shorter history, population loss induces a sort of civic panic and unleashes everything from government aid programs to thoughtful studies by academics and foundations. While by no means making light of urban decline, a little more perspective seems in order. Dan Kildee, an innovative civic leader from Flint, Michigan, has studied shrinkage in depth. "In Europe, because of their longer history, they don't blow a gasket when population goes down by 10 percent in a decade," he told me. "Their history showed their cities sort of *breathing*. Trends are longer; they take more time. In the United States we have one line up and one line down, and that's all we see."[4]

There's another reason why the self-defeating image of Rust Belt failure is out of whack with reality. The table below lists the twenty largest cities by population in 1960 and describes how those populations had changed by 2008.[5] One obvious trend is that most of the top twenty cities (twelve in all) lost

City	1960 population	Est. 2008 population	Percent gain/loss	Added land area?
New York	7,781,984	8,363,710	7	No
Chicago	3,550,404	2,853,114	-20	No
Los Angeles	2,479,015	3,833,995	55	Yes
Philadelphia	2,002,512	1,447,395	-28	No
Detroit	1,670,144	912,062	-45	No
Baltimore	939,024	636,919	-32	No
Houston	938,219	2,242,193	139	Yes
Cleveland	876,050	433,748	-50	No
Washington, D.C.	763,956	591,833	-23	No
St. Louis	750,026	354,361	-53	No
Milwaukee	741,324	604,477	-18	No
San Francisco	740,316	808,976	9	No
Boston	697,197	609,023	-13	No
Dallas	679,684	1,279,910	88	Yes
New Orleans	627,525	311,853	-50	No
Pittsburgh	604,332	310,037	-49	No
San Antonio	587,718	1,351,305	130	Yes
San Diego	573,224	1,279,329	123	Yes
Seattle	557,087	598,541	7	No
Buffalo	532,759	270,919	-49	No

people, often close to half their populations. Three other cities—New York, San Francisco, and Seattle—more or less held their own and today are within 10 percent of their population levels in 1960. Only five cities grew dramatically, and those cities—Los Angeles, Houston, Dallas, San Antonio, and San Diego—often more than doubled their population. But here's the tricky part: Those five cities also have added substantial land area since 1960. Houston doubled its land area over that time, while San Antonio tripled its size. How? Just like Dresden, they annexed their suburbs as they grew.

Cities—all cities—spread out following World War II, thinning the population density as people moved from crowded city brownstones to single-family houses on suburban lots. This means that those big-growth Sunbelt cities, whose laws allowed annexation, were gaining population not in their older central cores but out in the newer bedroom suburbs. Detroit and other heartland cities, hemmed in by a variety of legal and political restrictions, were never able to capture that natural suburban growth. Detroit grew to its current size of 139 square miles by the 1920s and has been landlocked ever since. Houston's land area today is six hundred square miles, while San Antonio's sprawls out over 412 square miles. Buffalo, meanwhile, occupies a tight forty square miles, while Boston covers forty-eight. While there was a shift to the Sunbelt in post–World War II America—the population surges in Florida, California, and Arizona are obvious—if we consider population decline in metropolitan areas in general, then places like Metro Detroit don't look nearly like the failures we picture them to be. In fact, Detroit's metropolitan population—city and suburbs combined— has grown since 1960 from 3.9 million to about 4.4 million today.

This may provide cold comfort to residents in places like Youngstown and Buffalo and Detroit. Noses pressed against the glass, looking at suburban growth, they feel more acutely than ever their own population loss. But seeing the trend for what it is and what's really at work might talk them and the rest of us down from the heights of despair. It isn't wise or practical to look at growth— population gains, bigger and better economic figures—as our only definition of urban success. We have to begin seeing—and believing—that smaller can mean better.

Doubtful? Let's explore the issue in more depth.

WHY SMALLER CAN MEAN BETTER

As a reporter covering urban development for the *Detroit Free Press*, occasionally I write about the "Best and Worst Places to Live" surveys that come out regularly. Most of these surveys treat Detroit badly, of course. *Forbes* magazine put Detroit at the top of its "Most Miserable Cities" list in 2008. Other lists, depending on their criteria, do much the same. Occasionally a "best list" will discover that southeast Michigan enjoys great universities and unparalleled access to fresh water, and rank the area higher. But generally, Detroiters know what to expect.

Scoff at these lists as we may, I think they contain a kernel of insight. These lists tell us, in a variety of ways, that smaller is better. On the *Forbes* "Most Miserable Cities" list, Chicago and New York—two of the most vibrant cities in the nation, mind you—also ranked high, based in part on long commute times. If longer commutes condemn a city to misery, then virtually no big city makes the cut. We see this smaller-is-better theme playing out in survey after survey. The annual "Best Places to Live" list compiled by *RelocateAmerica* includes, among its top ten cities, Durham, North Carolina, with 222,000 residents; Little Rock, Arkansas, with 185,000 people; and Huntsville, Alabama, with a population of 170,000.

Why do the people who rank cities think that smaller is better? If you read these surveys, you'll get the impression that smaller means a more affordable, community-minded, Earth-friendly environment with shorter commute times and a healthier atmosphere in which to raise families. On the other hand, in addition to long commute times, really big cities impose stress in the form of more expensive housing, high taxes, crime, pollution, noise, and a general lack of neighborliness. Of course, these surveys ignore the obvious trade-off: that large metropolitan areas also offer a cultural life and economic opportunities not available in smaller towns.

So our next question becomes this: If small is good, and maybe even better than big, why do we scold Detroit and Cleveland and Youngstown for *getting* smaller? Dan Kildee—whose jurisdiction as Genesee County treasurer included Flint, a city that has experienced shrinkage—argues that our perceptions need an adjustment. "There's nothing that says that the quality of life in a city is determined by the number of people who live there," he told me. If size alone mattered, then "nobody would want to live in Traverse City. Everybody would want to live in Detroit. So the measure of a community's quality or success is not the population figure. The measure is what is life like for whatever number of people choose to live there."

Of course, smaller towns like Huntsville and Traverse City tend to start small and grow to their current modest size, while Detroit and Cleveland and Youngstown began much larger and have been shrinking—a very different dynamic. Shrinkage has inflicted incredible pain on many cities. But as we can see, shrinkage—or spreading out, the term I prefer—is a natural phenomenon that happens everywhere. Houston's population has spread out from the original metropolitan core as the city has grown, just as the population of Metro Detroit has spread out as the city has grown, the only difference being that Detroit's natural impulse to spread out has been stifled by artificial boundary lines. In the Unites States alone, Kildee says, dozens of large cities can be described as shrinking. "This idea that we ought to ignore those [cities] and only consider them successful places if we somehow can turn around their population trend and have this major repopulation effort, it's a concept that requires far too many places to be failures," he says. "It just doesn't work."

But can a shrinking city like Detroit actually be *better* for being smaller? We won't know for certain until we see how events play out over the next ten or twenty years. But we do know this much: Being smaller affords opportunities that would have eluded Detroit in its supposed heyday of the 1950s. Take the greening movement. All sorts of people in Detroit today are fighting to make the city more Earth friendly. They're building greenways—paved or unpaved trails for bicyclists and other non-motorized modes of travel—using the city's vacant spaces as routes. Getting smaller means we can dig up some of the landscape that's been concreted by developers and uncover some of the natural features, with benefits that range from happier travelers to lower temperatures in the summer to cleaner air.

The city's vacant land can also serve another vital purpose: growing food. Our nation—indeed, the world—may be facing climate and energy crises that could disrupt our global food system. Detroit, like every other city in America, imports almost all of its food. But Detroit's significant amount of free land could be farmed in urban gardens for fruits and vegetables, creating an advantage in meeting any food-supply disruption that might occur, and its network of greenways could help residents get by without their cars.

A municipality whose budget is stretched to the breaking point may find that smaller means cost savings—fewer services to deliver to a smaller population. (Of course, city governments have to be smart in how they make the adjustment, not simply abandon services.) As Mayor Jay Williams of Youngstown says in the foreword to this book, a city getting smaller may gain flexibility to become more innovative. New ideas and approaches can be tested on a more manageable scale with quicker results.

Most intriguing of all, a city with significant open spaces like Detroit can think about reshaping its urban fabric—building up the stronger districts to be even healthier, and encouraging people to abandon the dying districts so the land there can be used for greenways or community gardens or other innovations.

Joan Nassauer, a professor of landscape architecture at the University of Michigan, told me she can see that sort of future for Detroit. "Honestly, a hundred years from now," she said, "I can imagine a city that has an even more extensive and accessible system of open space, but where Detroit's apparent advantages are so attractive that the parts of the city that are built upon are way more dense than they are now. It could be a city of two and a half million. It could be a city of four million, but with more open space and higher density in the developed areas."[6]

Denser than today in some areas, with bounteous open spaces in other parts of the city—that's one future made possible only by getting smaller for a time. Getting smaller opens up the possibility for something new to take place. A *smaller* city creates the canvas to become a *better* city.

For those who find such a prospect frightful, look no farther than the suburbs to see how delightful a less dense urban landscape can be. In many of the leafier suburbs all across America, the homes are set far back from the street, open fields surround schools, and landscaped medians separate traffic on many corridors. Indeed, the population density in Oakland County north of Detroit is less than *half* of what it is within the city limits even today. A posh suburb like Bloomfield Hills presents a very pleasant prospect indeed, but if we could transfer the same amount of open space to Detroit—take those same deep setbacks and the same wide spacing between occupied buildings, and overlay it on a Google Earth image of the city—we would find the suburban land use more or less matches what's left in Detroit today. Of course, in suburbia we find a *planned* emptiness. Suburban zoning codes have created a landscape of diffused development, of elbow room. In the city, the same emptiness came about through abandonment. Suburbs, too, enjoy the tax dollars to keep their emptiness looking pretty. Most big cities do not, and hence the dispiriting aspect of Detroit and so many other once-proud cities today. Given proper care, though, the empty fields in Detroit could look a whole lot better. Get rid of the dumped tires and the smashed liquor bottles, cut the grass, plant sunflowers, raise vegetables, install some art objects, and pretty soon the landscape doesn't look bleak at all. It looks hopeful, as if somebody cares.

A city getting smaller emerges from the agonies of shrinkage with the opportunity to become something new in a way that wasn't possible before. If a city getting smaller is willing to treat its condition as an opportunity and not as a reason for despair, there's no telling what it may accomplish.

Still not convinced? Let's look at two real-life examples.

Turin, Italy

Detroiters and residents of other distressed cities are seeking, naturally enough, examples of shrinking cities that have recovered and prospered. The vista in America is not very encouraging. Many skeptics point to ghost towns of the Old West as the only possible future for cities like Detroit. But we just need to look farther afield. There is a city that found the path to recovery, that completely turned its image of failure into one of success, and where recovery took less time than anyone had dared hope. Even better, the analogy with Detroit couldn't be more exact. That city is Turin, Italy, which for decades bore the uncanny nickname "The Detroit of Italy."

Turin, or *Torino* in Italian, nestles along the valley of the Po River with hundreds of kilometers of soaring Alpine peaks in the distance. Founded by the Romans a few decades before Christ's birth, Turin stood at the gateway to the broad northern Italian plain for travelers from what we now know as France. The city remained a center of local then regional power throughout the Middle Ages. As Italy's many autonomous states unified in the mid-nineteenth century, Turin served for a brief, heady time as the national capital city. The seat of government moved quickly to Rome, a blow to Turin's ego, but the city soon attracted much of Italy's nascent manufacturing industry. Turin became the headquarters and manufacturing center of Fiat, as well as the home of Lancia and Alfa Romeo. Allies bombed the city's factories during World War II, but the ground war spared Turin, and the city quickly recovered after the war. By 1980 or so, Turin boasted a population of 1.2 million and a seemingly bright future.

Then Turin's automobile industry collapsed just as Detroit's signature industry was imploding. Fiat almost died, and Turin lost roughly 25 percent of its population in less than twenty years. Empty factories marred the cityscape. Without a robust auto industry to underpin the city's economy, Turin took a good look at itself and saw what the rest of the world saw—a gray, grimy factory town that had lost any semblance of hope.

Then Turin shook off its despair and got to work. The city elected a new mayor, Dr. Valentino Castellani, a former telecommunications engineer, in 1993. Castellani undertook a broad-based strategic planning process for his city, involving powerful and ordinary citizens alike. At the first brainstorming session to which the public was invited, Castellani worried that nobody would show up; instead, an overflow crowd of several hundred people was left standing outside. "We had to manage the anger of those people, but it was much better than having to manage the failure," Castellani told me during a September 18, 2009, visit to Detroit.

So the city took stock. It dug into its past to find a way toward the future. Around 1900, Turin had been the home of Italy's first cinema productions, and after World War II an avid fan had collected many artifacts of that film industry. Now Turin used that collection to create the National Museum of Cinema. The city housed the new museum in the Mole Antonelliana, the city's tallest building and Turin's postcard image, built in the mid-1800s as a Jewish Synagogue but mostly empty and owned by the city for decades. The museum now draws almost a million visitors a year. Turin also began the Torino Film Festival for newer artists. It nurtured a special-effects and animation park, and created incentives to lure filmmakers. Many television shows and movies are shot in Turin now, and the city reaps the benefit of seeing itself and its Alpine background in movies and on TV.

The city also moved ahead with transportation plans, building the *Spina*, or spine, a miles-long north-south boulevard over what had been an open railroad trench. Turin has mapped plans for a new subway, with the first link already completed. The city, using the slogan "Passion Lives Here," bid for and won the right to host the XX Winter Olympics. Like all Italian cities, Turin takes pride in its food, and the city hosts an annual chocolate festival, during which tourists and residents are invited to visit the numerous chocolate-tasting stations, where chocolate is offered the way wine is offered in wine bars. Perhaps most significantly, the city stopped ignoring the Alps and started to promote itself as an Alpine city, a hub of European culture and travel.

This recovery took a tremendous amount of effort, Castellani told me. Political stability helped; he held the mayor's office for two four-year terms, and his chosen successor looks likely to hold it for another eight years. A region-wide planning process and a commitment to a bottom-up process that excluded no one were also key to the recovery. But all the efforts paid off. Turin's population has shown a modest recovery, adding about 5 percent more people since 2000, and the city now thinks of itself not as tired and old but as fresh and new and hopeful. "A crisis can be an extraordinary opportunity for change and innovation," Castellani said. "Paradoxically, the deeper the crisis, the bigger the chance to change and innovate."

Perhaps the most extraordinary thing about Turin's death-and-life experience is that it wasn't the first time the city had to reinvent itself. Remember how Turin lost the national capital in the 1860s? Castellani described that period as a time of great despair for the city. But Turin reinvented itself as the car-making capital of Italy. Now it's turned another corner and forged a new identity and a new future. "If you can find a way to move the energy," Castellani said, "it is unbelievable what you can accomplish."

A Detroit-area businesswoman named Beth Ardisana heard Castellani describe Turin's experience. Ardisana, president and CEO of ASG Renaissance, a Dearborn-based marketing firm, sums it up this way: "People once called Torino the Detroit of Italy. Our goal now is to call Detroit the Torino of the United States."[7]

The Youngstown Story

Like numerous shrinking cities in the United States, Youngstown saw its population peak in the 1950s. Never a truly large city, Youngstown enjoyed an outsized reputation as a major steel town, where the mills and smokestacks defined the local economy and carried the city's fame far and wide. Then, in September 1970, the steel mills began to close. Youngstown saw its population dwindle from a high of around 190,000 to 95,000 by 1990.

Like many such cities, Youngstown harbored dreams of getting it all back. The 2000 United States Census dashed those hopes. Youngstown's population had sunk to 82,000, a 14 percent drop from ten years earlier. It was the sharpest decline of any major Ohio city. A lot of people looked at the results and had the same epiphany—that Youngstown was never going to recover its lost people and jobs, and that something new and different needed to be done. The old dreams had died. What would take their place?

What emerged from the soul-searching was the Youngstown 2010 plan.[8] This new master plan for the city's future development accepted the reality of population loss. It asserted that Youngstown could be a great *smaller* city. It presumed that, with a smaller population, Youngstown didn't need as much urbanized land mass as it once had. So the plan mapped a future for Youngstown that called for large swathes of the city to be set aside for recreation and urban agriculture.

As modest as it was, the plan electrified the world of urban planning. It was the new vision that shrinking cities had been groping for, even if they hadn't known it yet. Pretty soon, planners, journalists, and scholars from as far away as The Netherlands and China were making the pilgrimage to Youngstown. And they all wanted to talk to one man, the city's new young mayor, Jay Williams.

Jay Williams grew up in Youngstown, went to work as a part-time bank teller as a young man, and worked his way up the bank chain of command. His passion was getting the bank to loan in city neighborhoods—not the sort of subprime loans that later caused so much trouble, but lending to credit-worthy borrowers. He got more and more involved in neighborhood economic development. A stint at the Federal Reserve Bank branch in Cleveland followed, and then Williams returned to Youngstown and became the city's development director.

That was just about the time that the results of the 2000 U.S. Census came out. "While the signs were all around us," Williams told me, "it just maybe was a sort of wakeup call. This notion . . . of waiting for the future, waiting for the steel mills, waiting for someone else to figure it out—we had waited for twenty, thirty years."[9]

As the city's development director, Williams got to work researching how to make Youngstown a better city. Youngstown 2010 didn't come off-the-shelf from consultants or warmed over from another city. Williams worked out the details in numerous meetings with residents. He is quick to credit the people of his city for the vision and the details of the plan. But if a lot of people deserve credit, Williams became the public face of the most innovative American civic plan in decades.

Williams found himself inspired by the new possibilities offered by the process of creating the Youngstown 2010 plan. He began to preach the notion that smaller could be better—that Youngstown with a smaller population might become easier to manage and govern, and that the quality of life could be good, too. Youngstown had been forced to stare into the mirror and stop denying what it had become. "There was this overriding inferiority complex," Williams recalled, and the new plan was meant to overcome that.

Youngstown 2010, like so many plans in so many cities, might have rested on a shelf forever. But in 2005, Williams, still only in his mid-thirties, decided to run for mayor. At first he was the longest of long shots. His primary opponents in 2005 offered the old formulas and more or less ignored what had emerged as the Youngstown 2010 plan. Williams ran in part to force the conversation to the issues of the plan. "It was not that I didn't plan to win," he said, "but [I] was obviously a long shot, having never held public office, and the party machine was doing its thing. But I knew that if I was in the race we would discuss the Youngstown 2010 issues."

Williams made the new plan the focus of his campaign. "I thought the other people who didn't campaign on this [platform] were crazy," he said. "There had been a great deal of civic trust invested in this process, and this is civic trust that had not been invested community-wide in anything for twenty years," he recalled. "So how could we then have a mayoral election and not have this be the topic of discussion and the focus?" Voters, it turns out, were way ahead of most politicians. Williams won handily and faced no serious opposition to his reelection bid in 2009.

Many outsiders don't get that Youngstown 2010 isn't a new version of the old urban renewal schemes of the 1950s and '60s, in which whole neighborhoods were bulldozed. The realization that Youngstown 2010 is something different hasn't sunk in yet. Journalists and planners from all over the world have found their way to Williams's city hall office, and the most common question—and the least helpful, really—is which parts of the city he planned to cut off and abandon. "People say, 'Okay, show us where you've cut the streets off and where you've moved all the people out,'" Williams told me. Instead, Youngstown 2010 envisions reshaping the city incrementally and voluntarily. There will be no use of eminent domain. The city will nudge now and then, providing incentives or withholding them to shape the behavior it wants. But if people want to stay right where they are, they're free to do so. The lights and heat will still come on, and the cops will still respond to a 911 call.

Three real-life examples give a flavor of what Youngstown hopes to accomplish and how it plans to get there. First, the city is applying some of its traditional aid programs in new ways, hoping to shift behavior in a different direction. Formerly Youngstown used some of its federal Housing and Urban Development block grant money to pay for home repairs for city residents. If a person qualified under income guidelines, then the application would be approved more or less automatically. "Now we're saying it may not make sense to invest fifty thousand dollars to renovate this home" in a dying neighborhood, Williams said. "So, Mrs. Jones, we would like to offer you a package that will allow you to relocate elsewhere in the city, make you whole, and are you interested in that?" If Mrs. Jones answers yes, then she'll get the incentives to move to her new location in a healthier neighborhood. If she declines, that's her choice, but the city won't provide the rehabilitation money it once did. "We're no longer going to offer a complete in-place rehabilitation," Williams said. "We're not going to force you out, but we'll move on to the next case. That is an evolution in our policy that I think people have mistaken" for forcing residents out of certain areas.

Take a second case: A contractor with a huge equipment yard where he assembles and repairs industrial equipment needs more room, so he's been buying up nearby houses as they become available. He's asked the city to consider vacating and closing off two or three streets once he owns all the houses there. Williams said the city is likely to grant the request. By trimming back the residential district in that part of town, the city saves money on services and puts underused land to a more productive use.

The third example may show more clearly than any other how Youngstown has rewritten its rulebook. A residential developer came in and requested the city's approval to build scatter-side residential units—that is, a house on a lot here and another there and so forth. The city always allowed such development in the past. In the early 1990s, when the low-income tax-credit housing boom began, the city agreed to it based on the theory that any new development was terrific. "Now when you look at it through the context of a plan, it didn't make sense," Williams told me. "First of all, we have a surplus of housing, so we've got to be careful about what we build. Second of all, it is going to be extremely important *where* you build, and we are not going to provide assistance to build houses where it doesn't make sense."

Under Youngstown 2010, the city tries to steer new residential development to the most viable and economically self-sustaining districts. Williams carefully avoids the adjective "better" to describe these neighborhoods because of the loaded value judgments inherent in the word. But it's clear Youngstown hopes to reinforce its stronger districts and not pour money into neighborhoods where it will do little or no good. Williams explained to me how the new policy confuses developers:

> We actually sent a letter down to the state capital to say this particular development is not consistent with our long-range development and we will not support it. And that developer did not receive the state tax credits. It caused a bit of conflict. It's not that we're not supporting you as a developer or development in the city, but they had become accustomed to buying lots, getting a standard form letter rubber-stamped by the city and going ahead and building because it generates their development fees. And now some of these houses they built ten years ago are vacant and boarded up. We'll actually try to force the issue, say, "We don't need your money. We will do what we need to do to prohibit you from developing in areas where it doesn't make sense." We're no longer accepting "It's new housing, so it must be good."

Williams told me that Youngstown 2010 will quickly evolve into Youngstown 2020—that the plan is a living document to carry the city into the future, not a fixed goal to be met by an artificial deadline. In the meantime, cities far and wide are looking to Youngstown to see how this former steel town manages the trickiest second act in urban America. "There's still a lot of work to be done," Williams said. "We haven't solved it. As these things get out there, the folklore begins to overtake the actual progress. But the fact that we're having this conversation in the city and amongst other cities I think is light-years from where we were."

2

DETROIT TODAY

To understand Detroit today, its uniqueness and its special challenges, it helps
first to visit a city like Philadelphia. During the summer of 2009, as I was writing
this book, I toured many of Philadelphia's distressed districts with a guide
named Bob Grossmann. Bob runs the vacant land restoration programs for
Philadelphia Green, which is the city's nonprofit tree-planting and community
gardening organization. In his younger days, he worked as an autoworker and
then as a builder before his love of gardening and volunteering led him to his
current job. As he drove me through several neighborhoods on Philadelphia's
north side, all of which have been scarred by poverty, the drug trade, and the
loss of jobs, we passed many signs of hope: small urban farm gardens and vacant
lots his group had rescued with clean-ups and fencing and regular maintenance.
While I did see some vacant buildings and peeling paint, I had expected much
worse from my tour—some collapse on the scale of what I see in Detroit. All
these Philadelphia districts looked surprisingly solid and even healthy to my
eyes. Brownstone buildings stood in unbroken ranks around many parks and
squares, and the vacant lots remained in the minority. The city showed good
bones. Philadelphia still looked *urban*.

Visiting similar at-risk districts in Detroit, the most striking characteristic
is the vacant feel of the city, those ghost streets with just one or two houses
left, those expanses of what Detroiters long since have taken to calling "urban
prairie." Detroit has lost roughly 50 percent of its population since the 1950s,
but Cleveland, Pittsburgh, Buffalo, and other cities have lost about the same
percentage, and St. Louis has lost even more; yet those other cities don't convey
this same emptiness and feeling of abandonment. There's a cable television
show called *Life After People* that, with computer-generated effects, illustrates
how nature will reclaim our great cities the moment we're gone. Grass will grow

in our streets and trees will take root inside buildings. Detroiters point out that nature already triumphs in many parts of their city today. Trees and overgrowth reclaim the vacant lots; wildflowers bloom amid the rubble; grass and weeds stand so tall and lush in July and August that a wanderer can feel overwhelmed with the creeping intensity of it all—*stifled in vegetation*, to borrow a phrase from Willa Cather's *My Ántonia*.

It's this scale of vacancy, these vast patches of rural landscape within a city of several hundred thousand residents, that defines Detroit's uniqueness among American cities. "This is probably the most significant vacant property problem in the country," Dan Kildee told me when I spoke with him on April 23, 2009, at the offices of the Genesee County Land Bank, of which he was chair. "I've visited virtually every city in America that has this problem," he said, "and no city has a more profound problem than Detroit."

One seasoned observer is Robin Boyle, chair of Wayne State University's Department of Geography and Urban Planning. Recruited to his post from his

Even downtown, vacancy abounds. Some of these lots on the northern edge of downtown were cleared for Super Bowl XL parking but remain awesomely empty most of the time. (Author photo)

native Scotland in the early '90s, Boyle says he was immediately struck by the uniqueness of Detroit's wide-open spaces. Those spaces resist normal planning, he told me in one of our many conversations. Dealing with voids within a city lies outside the experience and even the language of most urban planners, architects, and social scientists. Planners and architects build and manage growth, while social scientists—economists, sociologists, epidemiologists—learn to use data, mostly from the U.S. Census, to study, characterize, and help distressed residents. Nobody trains to deal with the emptiness other than by filling it with traditional development—housing, retail space, industrial parks—but that kind of development is inadequate to deal with the scope of Detroit's prairies.

In late 2009, Boyle challenged his Wayne State students to create innovative solutions to Detroit's vacancy. Think of the scale, Boyle urged his students. "I kept saying, 'A hundred-thirty-nine square miles,'" which is the land area of the city of Detroit. "I kept throwing that number up on the wall, a hundred-thirty-nine square miles: 'How does your prescription—wilderness or farming or neighborhood/village development—how does that assist in the hundred-thirty-nine square miles?'" But the monumental scale of the problem dwarfed the students' imaginations, and they turned in mostly block-and-neighborhood-level solutions.

"We had an argument one night on the Dequindre Cut," Boyle said, referring to one of Detroit's newest bicycle and strolling paths. His students saw the Dequindre Cut as a model project, but Boyle urged them to consider how difficult it would be to emulate the project throughout such a huge city. "I said, 'That's great, it's 1.3 miles at the cost of about one million dollars a mile or more. Expand that out. Think of the cost that would be.'" Boyle does believe, however, that Detroit has a chance for revival. "We're not going to give up," he said. "We're going to fight for it. There are enough people willing to fight for it. But I think their tools are blunt."[1]

Why does Detroit look so sparsely populated today when other cities equally stricken by population loss look so much better? "Better" may be a relative term; many parts of Chicago may look dreadful, but they look dreadful in an urban way, while Detroit slowly returns to nature. There are two reasons, I think, and again we'll look first to Philadelphia for comparison. There's a stretch in the northern section of Philadelphia along the Delaware River that once housed so many mills and factories that it gained fame as "The Workshop of the World." Stetson made hats there, just one of thousands of products churned out. When those businesses collapsed or moved out in the years after World War II, the hole each one left behind was relatively modest—an acre here, perhaps five acres there. But when Detroit lost its auto factories, many of which once employed thousands of men and women, it often lost a hundred acres of urban landscape at a crack. A lot of those empty factories still stand, most famously the Packard plant, the first great automotive manufacturing center of the early 1900s, abandoned now for decades. Everyone knows the Packard plant. It's the one with the trees growing from the roof and the slowly crumbling walls and the trash fires set weekly if not daily by vagrants and punks. But the city of Detroit razed a lot of other empty factories, and the gaping holes in the landscape today are numerous and large. When a tannery in Philadelphia closed down, it was possible for Bob Grossmann and Philadelphia Green to help residents build an urban park and a community garden to fill up the space. It's harder to do that when the vacant site measures a hundred times larger.

The second reason for Detroit's striking emptiness today is the quality of the city's housing stock. Detroiters boasted for generations of having the highest percentage of homeownership of any big city. The ability for working-class families to buy their own homes—and even to buy a fishing boat or a cottage up north—remained Detroit's proudest achievement throughout its Auto Century. But vast numbers of those working-class and middle-class houses sprang up so quickly that there wasn't time or space for the painstaking construction and deliberate planning we see in, say, the neighboring Grosse Pointe communities. For example, the city of Highland Park, a one-time farming village now contained entirely within Detroit's borders, mushroomed from four hundred residents in 1900 to forty thousand just twenty years later. While there are some wonderful Arts-and-Crafts bungalows in Highland Park, as there are good houses throughout Detroit, there are also many quickly built wooden houses that have not withstood time as well as the brownstones of Philadelphia and New York and Chicago.

Detroit, too, is a relatively humid place, nestled as it is alongside the Great Lakes, and the humidity is not kind to houses with wooden siding, especially when they don't get the upkeep they should. Detroiters also say the city has a high water table, meaning you can dig down just a couple of feet in many places to strike water. To be more precise, the glaciers that came through thousands of years ago left a dense layer of clay a couple of feet below the soil, so that rain and snowmelt doesn't percolate down easily. The water perches atop the surface of the clay, trapped there, so it's no surprise that wet basements are a problem throughout the city. Combine the hasty wood construction with a humid environment, then layer on poverty rates among the nation's worst, and the result is a city that loses many houses to decay. Metal strippers and arsonists worsen the problem many times over, but Detroit would be suffering a deteriorating housing stock even without them.

Without meaning to, civic leaders have contributed to the city's wide-open spaces by ambitiously demolishing many vacant structures in the expectation of new development, much of which never happens. In 1999, the city mapped plans for the I-94 Industrial Park, a project meant to spark an economic rebirth

Vacant houses, beyond repair in many cases, slowly rot across Detroit's landscape. (Author photo)

by attracting new companies. It was the old "build it and they will come" idea. The city bought and razed hundreds of houses, adding to property it already owned, creating a 189-acre development-ready park. You have to see 189 acres of vacant land in the middle of a big city to understand the term urban prairie. The problem, of course, is that only one building has been developed in the park, and the rest of the site remains awesomely empty.

This is the city that journalists and documentary makers come to see today. Detroit, poster child of urban decay, has always drawn journalists or filmmakers looking for gritty material, and Eminem's film *8 Mile*, shot in the city, no doubt increased the level of interest. But during the spring and summer of 2009, the visiting writers and photographers became a swarm. It seemed that everybody with a camera or a notebook wanted a piece of Detroit. Britain's BBC, America's PBS, filmmakers and journalists from France, Ireland, and Australia all came to town. Time Inc. bought a house in the city's West Village district from which to write a year-long blog on Detroit. Commonly these out-of-towners used to Google "Detroit" and then call up the resulting local experts to ask for tours of the city. I showed several around myself, careful always to show the vibrant areas like Eastern Market and Indian Village as well as the requested evidence of vacancy.

So many of these out-of-town visitors scamper around Detroit these days that a writer named Thomas Morton mocked them in *Vice*, an online magazine of journalism and commentary. Titled *"Something, Something, Something, Detroit: Lazy Journalists Love Pictures of Abandoned Stuff,"* Morton's piece skewered the obsession with "ruin porn" and the tendency for everyone to shoot the same clichéd images: "Detroit is being descended on by a plague of reporters. If you live on a block near one of the city's tens of thousands of abandoned buildings, you can't toss a chunk of Fordite without hitting some schmuck with a camera worth more than your house."[2]

In this city, contradictions await on almost every street. Eastern Market on the city's near-east side thrives as a center of the local food economy. On Saturday mornings, local farmers arrive as dawn is smearing the eastern sky, and thousands of shoppers stroll the stalls buying fresh fruits and vegetables. They linger over breakfast or lunch in the many cafés, smile at the music of street musicians, hunt for antiques and bottles of wine in the shops. Not long ago, the financially strapped city of Detroit turned over governance of Eastern Market to a nonprofit corporation. That move alone, and the hiring of an excellent manager named Dan Carmody to run the corporation, did wonders to spruce up the down-at-the-heels operation. Nonprofit foundations have been giving generously to renovate the historic market buildings, many of which date back a century. New loft apartments in old brick industrial buildings share the outer blocks with bakers, wholesale produce dealers, and meat packers. The towers of downtown Detroit glimmer in the morning sunlight less than a mile away, and the Market bustles with activity and promise and hope.

Yet just a few blocks farther to the east, many streets are silent and abandoned. Several of the blocks have few houses left, or just one house, or none at all. A French independent filmmaker named Florent Tillon, who filmed a documentary in Detroit in mid-2009, characterizes this emerging Detroit landscape of emptiness as the revenge of nature upon the corporate world.[3]

Many Detroit neighborhoods appear more rural than urban, like this expanse on the city's near-east side. (Author photo)

Here and there humans have left their spoor—pop cans and shards of bottles, broken television sets, an old couch or a small boat left by itself in a field or along a curb. Old tires pile up by the truckload, dumped by somebody too poor or lazy to dispose of them legally. In these empty spots on Detroit's map, a vacant house often collapses on itself (often with the help of arsonists) and nature gradually reclaims it, so that many of Detroit's emptiest stretches are dotted with mounds of debris overflowing with vegetation. Sometimes a visitor can spot the entire process in a single field, as if nature operated an assembly line—a pile of tires or a collapsed house in one spot, a similar pile partially covered by grasses but with the human debris still poking out in another, and finally a fully formed earthen mound that appears to be solely the work of nature.

Add up all the vacancy, and the usual estimate one hears is that about forty square miles of Detroit's 139-square-mile area stand vacant today. Dan Pitera, a professor of architecture at the University of Detroit Mercy, captured this empty

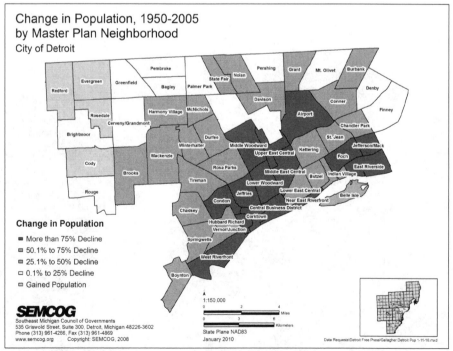

A half-century of population loss drained the inner heart of the city. (Courtesy Southeast Michigan Council of Governments)

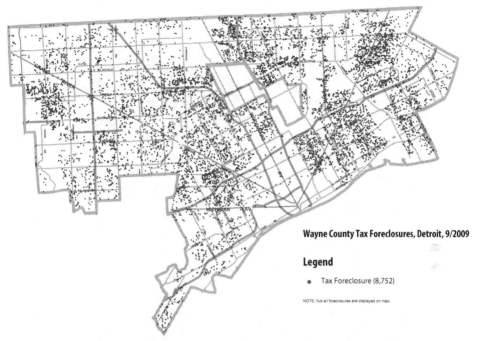

Wayne County Tax Foreclosures, Detroit, 9/2009

Legend

• Tax Foreclosure (8,752)

NOTE: Not all foreclosures are displayed on map.

Wayne County's tax foreclosure auction in late 2009 offered almost nine thousand properties for sale. Many were vacant lots. Yet even this number captures only a fraction of the vacant and abandoned parcels in Detroit. (Courtesy Detroit Vacant Property Campaign)

expanse brilliantly with a map showing how the landmass of Manhattan and the cities of San Francisco and Boston could fit entirely within Detroit's borders. Those three urban centers are home to a combined population of nearly three million people. When the *Detroit Free Press* reproduced Pitera's map on the front page,[4] the debate over what to do with Detroit's empty spaces landed on the kitchen tables of people all over the region.

Astonishingly, though, for a city so abandoned, the population density of Detroit today remains twice or more than that of sprawling Sunbelt cities such as Phoenix and Dallas. At its population peak in the 1950s, Detroit swelled with about thirteen thousand residents per square mile. Even today, with its population less than half its peak, Detroit still remains a crowded city by most standards, with about 6,500 residents per square mile. Phoenix boasts a comparatively sparse 2,900 residents per square mile and Dallas about 3,400 per square mile. Detroit's neighboring Oakland County to the immediate north, one

Comparing Detroit to three other major cities

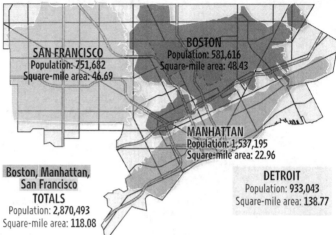

Dan Pitera's map as it appeared on the front page of the *Detroit Free Press.* The realization that entire cities could be dropped into Detroit with room to spare sparked new debate on what to do with Detroit's vacant spaces. (Courtesy Dan Pitera and *Detroit Free Press*)

SAN FRANCISCO
Population: 751,682
Square-mile area: 46.69

BOSTON
Population: 581,616
Square-mile area: 48.43

MANHATTAN
Population: 1,537,195
Square-mile area: 22.96

Boston, Manhattan, San Francisco
TOTALS
Population: 2,870,493
Square-mile area: 118.08

DETROIT
Population: 933,043
Square-mile area: 138.77

of the nation's wealthiest counties, fits in about 1,400 residents per square mile. Rural Livingston County to the northwest, which currently forms the outer edges of Detroit's suburban sprawl, boasts a rural-like three hundred people per square mile. Relatively speaking, Detroit is still densely occupied, but it's as if the old population density of the city and the gradually increasing suburban densities were destined to even out somewhere in the middle.

Indeed, many people describe Detroit as a new middle landscape, something between urban and rural. Others prefer the term "the new suburbanism" because in many ways the patterns of land use in Detroit have come to resemble suburbia. The very things many people enjoy about suburbia—the big backyards and the spacious setbacks that separate buildings from the roads and from each other—can now be found in Detroit, albeit by accident.

In many places around Detroit, we find residents who have reclaimed one or more of the vacant lots near their homes. Some have gone to the trouble to buy a vacant lot from the city's inventory. But since dealing with the dysfunctional city bureaucracy requires a degree of tenacity and patience beyond most of us, many people have simple squatted on the vacant properties, fencing them off or planting them as gardens. Three New York City–based designers, Tobias

Armborst, Daniel D'Oca, and Georgeen Theodore, dubbed these newly enlarged residential sites in the city "blots."[5] Many of Detroit's residential lots measure only thirty feet across and a hundred or so feet deep, developed long before attached two-and-three-car garages became standard. When an adjacent lot or two is added, the standard city lot begins to look like a suburban lot. Armborst, D'Oca, and Theodore found many different configurations of these newly expanded lots, including a simple one-plus-one, where a homeowner took over the lot next door, or cases where neighbors separated by two or more empty lots took them over in common and created a small fenced compound. Striking a hopeful note, the trio writes that the cumulative effect "will be a gradual rewriting of the city's genetic code: a large-scale, unplanned re-platting of the city that will happen through the bottom-up actions of thousands of individual homeowners."[6] Of course, this newly suburbanized landscape in Detroit will be gradual, unplanned, and uncoordinated, and the total impact is yet to be seen.

When Alan Mallach, an urban planner and the research director of the National Housing Institute in Montclair, New Jersey, led a team of experts to study Detroit in the later half of 2008, he concluded that Detroit was fragmenting and dissolving into a lumpy urban porridge, with areas of concentration surrounded by areas of much lower density. Mallach used the term "urban villages" to describe the more vibrant districts in the city. In one of the conversations we shared, I suggested that what Mallach was describing is what most people think of as a county—suburban villages surrounded by rural space. Mallach opted for the imagery of the English countryside. "In England they have very strict land-use rules," he explained. "The basic idea is you have no right to develop." Landowners only have the right to use land in whatever way it's been used before. "So government imposes very strict growth boundaries and only permits development when it's a logical extension of an existing village," Mallach said. "It's fabulous because you have high-density development on one side of the street and cows on the other, quite literally. And so you have this very strong pattern of built-up village, green space, farms, fields, forests, whatever for however long, then the next village, and only a few miles from each other."[7] In thinking about Detroit's future, Mallach suggested, think of it as a twenty-first-century version of a traditional country pattern.

When I wrote about Mallach's suggestion for the *Detroit Free Press*,[8] there was some good-natured joshing about English country villages and the Shires of Detroit, suggesting something out of *The Lord of the Rings*. But at bottom, Mallach was offering a very modern, even futuristic, vision of the city. The individual nodes of activity (think, say, the area surrounding Mexicantown in southwest Detroit where Latino immigrants have produced one of the few districts to gain population in recent years) would all be connected by transit lines. The areas of less activity in between could be converted to many uses— urban agriculture or recreation or wildlife corridors or wind farms or any number of other things.

For those who found Mallach's ideas fanciful or worse, he had a quick answer.

> Isn't that basically what's happening? Even without any plans or strategies? And in a sense it really is. But the problem is it's happening in a sloppy, destructive fashion, where you end up with the worst of both worlds. You get areas that are essentially abandoned, but they're not useable open space, they're not environmentally sound, so they're basically wasteland. And then because you don't have any policies to strengthen the nodes, you're having the areas that are still surviving and could be not only viable but thriving neighborhoods are being undermined by the population loss and the impoverishment and everything else. So in that sense, Detroit is moving to a pattern of nodes and open space, but because there's no plan and there's no strategy, they're moving to it in a way that is destructive in terms of the environment, the quality of life, the economy, and everything else, instead of moving to it in a way where it could be constructive and positive.[9]

DYSFUNCTION, DETROIT-STYLE

At this point, we can reasonably ask why Detroit hasn't done more about its problems. Detroit may rank at the wrong end of so many indices of urban woe—poverty, illiteracy, crime—but it also does less about those problems than other cities. Cleveland is way ahead of Detroit on its vacant land planning, while Pittsburgh has largely shaken off its loss of steel-industry jobs and based its economy on health care and education. Flint, a gritty automotive town that suffered at least as much abandonment as Detroit, is widely viewed as a leader for creating the nation's model land bank. Youngstown, Ohio, as we saw, leads the way in planning to be a better, smaller city.

Detroit has failed for years to address its problems, never more so than during the chaotic months of 2008 and 2009, when Mayor Kwame Kilpatrick—he of the infamous text messages to and from his chief-of-staff Christine Beatty—battled unsuccessfully to stay out of jail. At the same time, the city council all but fumbled away the city's signature annual auto show by stalling on a deal to upgrade the Cobo Center convention facilities. When rain leaked onto the floor during one event at Cobo, city council President Pro Tem Monica Conyers (who herself would shortly plead guilty in a bribery scheme) said it was a bid to win sympathy for the Cobo renovations.[10] The low point came when council member Barbara-Rose Collins broke into a rendition of "Onward Christian Soldiers" at the council table, leading columnist Nolan Finley of *The Detroit News* to say Detroit was being led by "lunatics and crazy old ladies."[11]

But the incompetence has been going on for years. In the 1990s, the U.S. Department of Housing and Urban Development made Detroit the first city to be cut off from a portion of HUD's largest home repair program, known as HOME, because of quality problems with repairs. The *Detroit Free Press* found that Detroit's HOME program had received $80.5 million between 1992 and 1998, yet only $26 million had been spent, and just 448 homes had been repaired or built.[12] Another outside study in the late '90s criticized the city's demolition of vacant houses, finding that Detroit's demolition program was hurt by a seriously fragmented administrative structure, and the cost of demolishing vacant homes had doubled in ten years.[13] The scandals continued into the new century. In 2003, federal judge placed Detroit's police department under a federal watchdog because the city's police killed too many people and arrested witnesses without probable cause. Even that federal oversight turned into a fiasco when the court-appointed watchdog couldn't or wouldn't account for millions of dollars in work billed to the city.[14]

Detroit, of course, has no monopoly on either incompetence or corruption. It may be, however, the only big U.S. city to be left almost entirely dysfunctional by its failings. In 2009, a Harvard professor of environmental economics named John Briscoe spoke in Detroit and mentioned that Brazilians have an expression in Portuguese, *rouba mas faz*, meaning "he steals, but he does" or "he steals, but he produces results." In many cities (Chicago, say), corrupt pols fling that justification at their critics, but Detroiters lack even that excuse. Many Detroit politicians steal but get nothing done.

One certainly gets weary dwelling on the various flavors of Detroit's dysfunction. But since dealing with vacant land plays such an important role in this book, I want to focus on one particular example before moving on.

DEALING WITH VACANT LAND

Margaret Dewar was a freshly minted urban planner working in Minneapolis/ St. Paul when she first hearkened to the call of Detroit. This was in the 1980s, and the young academic at the University of Minnesota was studying poverty in that state's more sparsely settled regions. All the while, though, she hungered for a different challenge. "I came into planning to work on issues of troubled industries, high poverty areas, regions in decline," Dewar told me February 18, 2009, in her office at the University of Michigan, where she's worked for many years. "When I was in Minnesota I worked on rural decline. When coming here I thought, 'I'm an urban planner, not a rural planner.'"

To an urban planner interested in urban decline and troubled neighborhoods, Detroit offered, even in the late 1980s, more grist that just about anywhere. Today, after twenty years of walking Detroit neighborhoods and talking to its people, Dewar still finds excitement in the city and its challenges. "It's a city of so many opportunities and so many challenges combined, and it's very exciting for an urban planner to work on and very enlightening," she said to me. "So it's wonderful for our students to cut their teeth on this. They become planners by working on Detroit issues."

Dewar typically will work with community partners—leaders of neighborhood associations, community development corporations, and other nonprofits—to develop a project for her graduate students that advances community agendas in a neighborhood. Detroit's hard-hit Brightmoor district on the northwest side was one recent focus. Her students talk, listen, ask many questions, analyze data, and come up with strategies for turning things around. The students share these plans with residents of the neighborhood and, if anyone at city hall is listening, with city officials.

By the late '90s, Dewar was pondering a question that struck her as odd.

All cities take control of vacant, abandoned, and tax-delinquent properties, and all cities try to put those parcels back into circulation as quickly as possible, usually by selling them to developers or nonprofit groups or even neighbors who will put the site back onto the tax rolls and into productive use. Dewar had long suspected that Detroit bungled this process more than most cities; the evidence was all around her as she walked the city. She thought this was just the reality in a city with weak demand for land, until she went to Cleveland and saw what nonprofit developers had done with land they acquired from the city. So she designed a study to compare how Cleveland and Detroit each disposed of city-owned parcels seized for unpaid property taxes. She obtained the land records of both cities, and drew each parcel's history from tax rolls and other databases. To follow up on what happened after each city disposed of its tax-reverted land, she drew two hundred properties at random from each city's list and visited each one to assess the condition. She interviewed city officials, nonprofit activists, developers, neighbors.

Dewar's results, published in the prestigious *Journal of the American Planning Association*, offer an appalling indictment of Detroit's mangled stewardship of land.[15] Fifty-two percent of the parcels that Cleveland sold became part of new projects in that city; in Detroit, the figure was 9.6 percent. Cleveland created a clear written policy for disposing of tax-reverted land. Detroit's land-disposition process was "opaque and changeable," Dewar wrote. Factional infighting between mayor and city council, and city and Wayne County often scuttled attempts at clarifying the process. Better policies developed during one mayoral administration in Detroit were often scrapped by the next mayor.

Ohio's property tax foreclosure and land bank laws meant that land bank property had clear title, while Detroit sold land without clearing title. That forced any developer or neighbor to spend considerable effort in clearing title before they committed to buying the city-owned property, and new owners were often unable to obtain a bank loan because of the danger of a previously existing claim to the site. Both Cleveland and Detroit issued holding letters to developers, giving them rights to certain parcels while they tried to put deals together. But Cleveland had a clear system for keeping track of these, while Detroit did not. When a project died in Detroit, no one would remove the "hold," so that during

Dewar's study, close to two-thirds of the city's land inventory was subject to holding letters. At the same time, Detroit sometimes gave one developer a holding letter yet sold the same parcel to somebody else. Cleveland's system for pricing land was clear and designed to sell the land quickly. In Detroit, prices for city-owned land were both unpredictable and much higher than in Cleveland. Even the simple act of learning how to buy a city-owned parcel and for what price required in Detroit an almost superhuman stamina and endurance, so intractable was the bureaucracy.

Viewed in isolation, Dewar's findings might strike us as the inevitable outcome of a city losing half its population since 1950. But Cleveland has lost half its population, too; as Dewar points out in her study, Detroit's 1950–2000 population drop of 48.6 percent almost exactly matched Cleveland's loss of 47.7 percent. The percent of city residents in poverty in 1999 was exactly the same for both cities: 25.6 percent. It's true that Detroit had a lot more vacant land to deal with than Cleveland, the result of a much higher population to begin with. (The percentage of decline was the same but the absolute number of parcels much higher in Detroit.) But that alone cannot explain so wide a discrepancy in outcome.

What does explain it? Numerous people have puzzled over Detroit's dysfunctional culture and offered explanations ranging from the city's poisonous race relations to the role of the federal government in subsidizing suburban growth in the 1950s. Let's examine another possible root cause—one that goes back to the early years of the twentieth century.

THE AUTO CENTURY AND ITS PERILS

Ben Hecht, the great screenwriter of Hollywood's early decades, wrote of his days as a foreign correspondent for a Chicago newspaper, living it up and staying in fine hotels on his newspaper's expense account in post–World War I Europe. When he finally came home to Chicago, he wrote, he was a pauper confirmed in the ways of a millionaire. That's Detroit's story. No boomtown ever boomed so long or so hugely as Detroit, and the city never got over it. The ride began, we might say, in 1914 when Henry Ford announced his five-dollars-a-day wage for factory workers; it didn't end, finally and decisively, until 2009 with the bankruptcy filings of General Motors and Chrysler. The end had been coming for decades, of course, at least since the 1970s, when small, fuel-efficient European and Japanese cars began to outsell domestic gas guzzlers. But reluctance to accept that changing model saw Detroiters clinging to a belief in their own privileged status long after it was justified.

The auto industry proved a boon for Detroit, but it exacted a toll, too. The men and women who built the cars, both on the line and in the front office, grew calluses on their hands and on their souls. Labor-management struggles led to a culture of conflict in all sorts of negotiations and relationships far from the factory floor. The fractious nature of city-suburban relations in recent years mirrors what had been taking place for decades in the auto plants. It was telling that the city's first black mayor, Coleman A. Young, came to public life not as a preacher of nonviolence like many civil rights leaders of his era but as a combative community and labor organizer.

In this culture of distrust and suspicion, if somebody offered you something, you rejected it out of hand, since only chumps accepted a first offer. Conversely, if somebody withheld something in negotiations, that something must be the real deal and a thing you deserved by right. The city and region convulsed at regular intervals as these union-management struggles erupted into prolonged strikes. The United Auto Workers union shut down General Motors for 113 days in 1945–46 and again for fifty-four days as late as 1998.

Ironically, both workers and management grew fat within this system, at least until the imports arrived. The car companies' huge profits in the 1950s and '60s showered wealth on shareholders and workers alike. Yet the generous lifestyle, unheard of for past American working-class families, fed a belief that it would never end. That belief in the omnipotent and bountiful automotive giants bled into many other areas of life in the city. It fostered a sense of entitlement and a sense of denial when harder times knocked at the door. What else explains the grotesque greed of a Kwame Kilpatrick or a Monica Conyers but a belief in their own deservedness? What else explains the reluctance of the city's municipal unions in mid-2009 to face the reality that the city was broke?

Sue Mosey, the longtime head of the nonprofit University Cultural Center Association, which works to rebuild the city's Midtown district, told me this sense of entitlement holds back needed progress even today, long after Detroit's woes became clear to all the world. "The reality is, Detroit has to quit thinking like Detroit's still the center of the universe, even in the Metro area, because nobody's buying that except the politicos downtown," she said. "Even redeveloping a neighborhood like this, we hold no delusions that there aren't plenty of other urban-style neighborhoods all around that are ahead of where we are, and where people make choices to live because the city services are better. That's just the reality."[16]

Detroit today is not unlike the cities in Europe following World War II. Those war-ravaged cities rebuilt themselves. Berlin was hollowed out by Allied attacks during the war; today Berlin thrives as a marvel of cosmopolitan energy. We enjoy something of that same opportunity here in Motown. No other city in America offers so vast a canvas for new thinking as Detroit.

It's time to speak of solutions.

POTENTIAL AND PROBLEMS IN
URBAN AGRICULTURE

If your image of a farm is something out of Iowa, endless rows of corn harvested by a Megalosaurus-sized combine, you need to visit the Norris Square district of Philadelphia and meet a woman named Iris Brown. Iris (pronounced *Ir-ez*) tends a garden known as *Las Parcelas*, which is Spanish for "The Parcels." Better than any other community garden in America, Iris Brown's blooming patch of land demonstrates how growing food inside a city can work the urban equivalent of a miracle.[1]

Brown is a small woman, born in a tiny village in Puerto Rico. Around Norris Square, she is called *La Jardinera* ("The Gardener"); she is also the best known of the neighborhood's *motivos* ("the motivated ones"), Puerto Rican women who speak little or no English but who brought the traditions of growing and cooking food in Puerto Rico with them to create urban gardens in their new home.

A few generations ago, Norris Square prospered as a workingman's district, filled with immigrant English, Scottish, Irish, and German weavers who worked in the local textile mills. In a pattern repeated nationwide, the mills closed after World War II, and middle-class families fled to the suburbs. Empty factories and vacant lots strewn with the detritus of urban life came to define the district. Drug dealers took over the street corners in what Philadelphians nicknamed "The Badlands." In 1985, the residents of the neighborhood—a mix of Puerto Ricans, Cubans, Dominicans, African Americans, and some Anglos—formed the United Neighbors Against Drugs, and every evening, crowds of them, twenty to forty at a time, walked the district and stood on street corners where drug deals flourished. Eventually the dealers moved on to more hospitable streets. Then the neighborhood enlisted the aid of Philadelphia Green, the nonprofit greening organization set up by the nearly two-centuries-old Pennsylvania Horticultural

Society. Philadelphia Green began to deliver help in the form of trees, plants, seeds, tools, money, and technical assistance.

Of the many gardens created in Norris Square with Philadelphia Green's help, Iris Brown's Las Parcelas became the centerpiece. Dedicated in 1993, it initially boasted sixteen family vegetable plots; today, that number has expanded to about forty, some tended by individuals, others by organizations. Some of

The Spring Garden urban farm in Philadelphia. (Courtesy Philadelphia Green)

the produce goes to City Harvest, the nonprofit organization that channels the output of urban gardens into local food banks. But growing food is only part of what Las Parcelas does for its neighborhood.

From the beginning, Brown saw Las Parcelas as a celebration—of many cultures, of music and dance and art, of children and their hopes. First she built La Casita, a replica of a rural Puerto Rican home circa 1940, to teach the local children about their island heritage. More recently, she added three small huts designed to replicate a chief's enclave in a West African village. On the day I visited Las Parcelas, Brown showed me through these joyfully colored huts and explained her goal in building them. "What we want to do is to have a space where we teach horticulture but, as important, the culture," she said. "Puerto Ricans, we are part African also, part European, and part native." She told me her people tend to acknowledge their European ancestry easily, their native Taino Indian blood less easily, and their African ancestry most reluctantly. "There's the hope the new generation will learn and then feel comfortable with who they are and celebrate who they are," she said.

As we explored further, Brown showed me other wonderfully crafted replicas of native architecture she had built at Las Parcelas using scrap wood from the neighborhood. One of the newest held a storytelling room decorated by the local children. There they draw and write in journals and make up games to play. "It's a little bit of many things in here," she said. Vibrant colors splashed everywhere. A hand-lettered sign read, "Without Tradition You Have Nothing." Brown explained why the buildings of Las Parcelas are so brilliantly painted. "This is for the people in the neighborhood," she said. "With the colors, hopefully they will get inspired."

Surrounding it all were the vegetable and herb plots. Brown grew up with the herbs of her native island, and she has long nurtured a design to grow as many of those Puerto Rican herbs and vegetables as she can in Philadelphia soil. "I come from a very small town in Puerto Rico," she told me, and there she learned African as well as Puerto Rican cooking and healing. "It's a very poor place, but we celebrate through music and dance and cooking." This year at Las Parcelas, they will cook using African herbs to keep the traditions alive.

Back in 1993, when a city councilman named Dan McElhatton helped dedicate Las Parcelas, he noted that he was an elected official but that Iris Brown was a leader.

A SHORT HISTORY OF FARMING INSIDE CITIES

Of all the innovative solutions offered to solve Detroit's problems, none has generated such enthusiasm, or so much skepticism, as urban agriculture. Advocates proclaim that farming inside cities will free us from the bondage of bad food and corporate greed, while others imagine we'll fill up Detroit's vast empty spaces with waving fields of wind-whipped wheat. Detractors, however, find the whole idea of growing food inside cities a joke. Even dedicated city planners often treat community gardens as a quaint temporary solution to vacancy. So in this chapter we'll examine both urban agriculture's great possibilities and the many obstacles that lie in the way of such a project reaching its full potential in places like Detroit. To tip my hand up front, I believe urban agriculture will play a critical role in Detroit's recovery, but I foresee multiple problems that we need to solve first.

To begin with, the whole notion of farming inside cities sounds like a contradiction in terms. We expect farmers to grow crops out in the countryside or perhaps on the urban fringes where a few pumpkin patches or apple orchards survive the onslaught of the bulldozers. Cities, on the other hand, are filled with asphalt and concrete and tall buildings and traffic jams. The urban farms that we see sprouting in cities across America today (and elsewhere in the world) strike many people as curiosities, perhaps akin to the plants we see growing up out of the cracks in sidewalks, or those trees that famously grow on the rooftops of Detroit's abandoned auto factories.

But farming inside cities, if you'll forgive the pun, has deep roots. People have been growing food on vacant lots and in city backyards and alongside urban schools and prisons and hospitals for more than a century. Laura Lawson, a professor of urban planning at the University of Illinois at Urbana–Champaign who studies community gardens, has identified six distinct phases of farming inside cities.[2] Ironically, given the importance of community gardens for the Motor City's future, some of the earliest and most vibrant examples of urban agriculture took place in Detroit.

The United States suffered a severe economic depression between 1893 and 1897, and Detroit's famous progressive mayor, Hazen Pingree, suggested the creation of urban gardens to give the unemployed and their families something useful to do. These garden plots became know as Pingree Potato Patches, and their popularity spread quickly. Nearly a thousand families participated the first year, farming on some 430 acres of loaned land, and each family's little quarter-acre or half-acre plot added up to a lot of food. What the families didn't eat was sold as surplus, and the whole operation reaped four times as much money as it cost to set it up with seeds and other supplies. Pingree launched that first effort in 1894, and by 1895 twenty other cities were creating their own urban gardens, including New York, Boston, and Chicago.

Right from the very beginning, we can see themes emerging that mark urban farming to this day. The community turned to urban gardening in response to a crisis, specifically an economic crash. That's true, today, too. Another trend we see repeated today: Those earliest gardening movements satisfied the latest thinking about how to help the poor. Those potato patches helped the needy help themselves so they would be less dependent on charity. And farming, backers believed, would teach traditional American values thought to be found in country life and strenuous outdoor activity, leaving little time to sulk and join labor unions or socialist societies. To some degree, the movement today touting self-reliance, physical activity, and healthful food echoes this earlier philosophy.

This melding of food production with social motivation remains central to community gardening. Even to this day, community farming is always as much about *community* as it is about *gardening*. Many of today's community farmers start planting their seeds as a way to improve the look of an abandoned city lot or empty building. And community gardening is the vehicle of choice to help all manner of distressed people—paroled prisoners and battered women and at-risk school children and the newest wave of immigrants to our shores. This is not to imply that farming inside cities doesn't produce a lot of food. It does. But if farming on a ten-thousand-acre farm in Iowa is all about producing the maximum yield for maximum profit, farming inside cities is not about profit at all, except at the far margins. It's about helping people—all manner of people in all manner of places—by providing food that is fresh, local, and free.

Overlapping in time with the Pingree Potato Patches was the birth of the School Garden Movement. The first U.S. school garden was founded at the Putnam School in Boston in 1891 and kicked off a national School Garden Movement that continued for a quarter century. Just as Pingree Patches drew on current thinking about how to help the poor, the School Garden Movement marked a rebellion against book learning in favor of hands-on, real-life experience. Growing vegetables, so the thinking ran, would stiffen the moral fiber urban children needed for the industrial jobs they would hold when they grew up. And gardening by school children created revenue in a way society deemed more acceptable than using child labor in factories. Gardening, Laura Lawson writes, "was particularly appealing as a way to teach appropriate social behavior to immigrants, delinquents, and the infirm."[3]

A photograph from the DeWitt Clinton Farm School in New York in 1902 gives an idea of both the scope of some of these school gardens and the ideals that motivated them. Substantial buildings flank two sides of the multi-acre field, and a tall fence encloses the other two sides, forming a secure border. In the middle of the rows and rows of vegetables towers an American flag. The whole scene suggests an attempt to protect children against the dangerous ideas floating just outside the compound.

Historically, another crisis brought another surge in urban gardening. When America entered World War I, people began to grow their own food again so that more U.S. produce could be sent oversees as part of hunger relief missions. The government encouraged it, but so did women's clubs and philanthropic societies. Farming inside cities became patriotic. Slogans like "Hoe for Liberty" and "Plant for Freedom" encouraged everyone to get involved. Gardening took on a democratizing air that, so people believed, would set workers and bosses on an equal footing. Americans grew so enthused that often they plowed under golf courses and other public spaces, to some people's dismay. At the end of the war, interest in the gardens began to slide, and the philanthropists and other supporters moved on to new causes.

The Great Depression changed that. Community gardening came back, often as part of relief packages offered by government or private companies. New York State reported that it had found more than sixty thousand subsistence gardens in backyards and vacant lots. Goodrich Tire Company and International Harvester set up gardens for workers to make up for lower pay and layoffs.

Then came World War II. Just as Detroit factories churned out more tanks and airplanes than anyone might have imagined, Americans grew an astonishing amount of food in their Victory Gardens. At their peak, those Victory Gardens produced 42 percent of America's vegetables during the war, freeing up a huge amount of more traditionally grown produce to go overseas. Among the benefits cited for this great surge in urban farming were a healthier diet, outdoor exercise, and distraction from worrying about the war. (Anyone who has ever sunk hands into dirt to plant a seed or weed a plot knows it's a natural stress buster.) Most Victory Garden plots were put to other use with the coming of peace, but a few survived, such as Fenway Community Garden in Boston.

There was another lull following World War II, and then the current era of urban gardening began to take root in the 1970s. The motives for the revival of farming inside cities remain an amalgam of traditional and new concerns. A shaky economy, the loss of industrial jobs, the abandonment of cities, the multiplication of vacant lots in dozens of proud cities nationwide—all these factors generated new interest in an old activity. So, too, did the backlash against corporate abuses and financial corruption in American life. Some community gardeners sought a simpler, purer way of life. Many people turned to community gardening to assert some control over their lives. It happened in cities all over America. In Detroit, the great activist Grace Lee Boggs, champion of the rights of women, people of color, and workers, started a local food movement around 1990 with friends who called themselves "Gardening Angels." Even more recently, concerns over climate change and global warming created still more urban farmers; these were city residents who wanted to live off the grid in some small way. And many people found that vegetables grown and picked just down the block offered more flavor than veggies shipped from thousands of miles away.

The burgeoning local food movement that now flourishes in cities across America remains small potatoes compared to what takes places beyond U.S. borders. Jerry Kaufman and Martin Bailkey, two researchers who have looked closely at the urban farming phenomenon, reported in a 2000 paper that food produced in cities accounted for 15 percent of the world's food production.[4] The government of Singapore was licensing almost ten thousand urban farmers who worked more than 17,300 acres of land, or a total of twenty-seven square miles. Those Singapore farmers produced 80 percent of the poultry and one-quarter of the vegetables consumed locally. Statistics like that show that producing food inside cities stands as a significant activity across many cultures. But there's a final example of farming inside cities, one often cited as the world's best example of its kind, that we need to see before looking at American urban farming in more detail.

How Havana Did It

Up until 1989, the island of Cuba owed much of its prosperity to being Moscow's thorn in America's side. The Soviet Union was eager to promote the image of a socialist paradise on the doorstep of the United States and spared no expense in doing so. The USSR and East Germany bought sugar from Cuba, paying prices well above market, and supplied Cuba with plenty of wheat and other food staples as well as farm and industrial equipment. Then the Cold War ended, Communism collapsed, and all the subsidized goods Cuba had been enjoying for years stopped coming.[5]

What followed was a large-scale test of what happens when a modern economy quits its subsidized existence cold turkey. Food supplies in Cuba dropped drastically, as other nations followed the Soviets' lead. The United Nations Food and Agriculture Organization reported that in 1989 the average Cuban was eating three thousand calories a day. By 1993, the figure had dropped to 1,900—crash dieting with a vengeance.

But during what become known as the "Special Period," Cubans reacted in a remarkable way. Instead of descending into civil chaos, average citizens started growing their own food. They planted vegetables and fruits on tiny plots all over the island, including in Havana and other cities. It was simple farming, without modern fertilizers and chemicals, since those modern agricultural inputs were no longer available. Pretty soon, by trial and error, Cubans built up their food supply again, and their average daily calorie intake gradually returned to 1989 levels.

Havana currently has more than two hundred of the small urban gardens known as *organoponicos*. These plots yield an astonishing amount of produce— about 300,000 tons of food a year, or nearly the entire vegetable supply for the city. To put that in perspective, Detroit's urban gardeners, who are among the most numerous and productive in any American city, grew about 165 tons of food in a recent year. So Havana farmers are producing roughly two thousand times as much food per year in their urban gardens as the growers in perhaps the most productive urban farming environment in the United States.

One obvious lesson from Havana's story is that a city can produce a lot of its own food when it puts its mind to it. Another is that urban farming contains the seeds of a new prosperity; in Havana, at least, thousands of urban gardeners make a modest income either selling their produce or being part of cooperatives that sell it. And a third possible lesson—one that many urban gardeners in places like Detroit are taking to heart—is that a city can live "off the grid" to a much greater extent than our modern agricultural economy would seem to permit.

That last point—that urban gardening enhances the independence of urban gardeners, freeing them from the clutches of the giant agribusinesses that dominate the food economy—is what makes the story of Havana during the Special Period so compelling. I first heard the story of Havana's urban farms at a video screening one evening in a shed at Detroit's Eastern Market. There were only about twenty of us there that evening under the high ceiling. Computer glitches delayed the video, and the sound was a little hollow. It was not, in other words, a slick presentation. But the message of a city relying on its own soil and its own citizens to grow its food proved powerfully moving.

Detroit, many say, is a "food desert." While the city offers its residents food on almost every busy street—indeed, obesity remains a major health concern in Detroit as elsewhere in America—it's the lack of fresh fruits and vegetables, as well as food products like canned tomatoes and fresh meats and fish, that is most disturbing. The paucity of grocery stores and the lack of a decent public transportation system condemn many Detroiters to buying whatever food they can find in corner liquor stores and the like. Often it's no better than microwavable tacos loaded with fat, sodium, and preservatives.

Charities in Detroit fill part of this nutritional gap by operating food banks or delivering fresh produce to the neighborhoods by truck; one such program in Detroit is the church-sponsored Peaches & Greens effort. Creating access to nutritious food for all urban residents remains the top goal of the community gardening movement. Many urban gardeners bring to their patches of dirt a deep commitment to social change, a shared goal of healing the environment and the food system. Understand that and we understand why so many urban gardeners refer to their movement with the phrase "food justice."

URBAN FARMING TODAY

If Las Parcelas ranks among the most remarkable of America's thousands of urban farms, many others offer equally inspiring stories. In 1995, a suburban farmer named Will Allen started a community garden in the city of Milwaukee with almost no money.[6] After earning a BA in 1971 from the University of Miami, Allen had played pro basketball for a few years and then put in time in corporate marketing for Procter & Gamble. But his roots eventually drew him back to farming. His goal in starting the organization now known as Growing Power was to give inner-city youth life skills by teaching them how to grow and sell organic produce. This youth-centered operation blossomed into multiple enterprises producing vegetables, cut flowers, and tilapia fish waste and worms for compost-making. The food produced by Growing Power is mostly donated to local food banks.

From his home base on two acres of land in Milwaukee, Allen oversees a constantly expanding and evolving network of efforts, partnering with local organizations to deliver food packages to the poor and running training seminars nationwide for youth and adults who want to bring fresh, healthy food to their inner-city communities. Spin-offs of Growing Power now operate in Chicago, where I visited one of its demonstration gardens in Grant Park, just steps from busy Michigan Avenue. "If people can grow safe, healthy, affordable food," Allen says, "if they have access to land and clean water, this is transformative on every level in a community. I believe we cannot have healthy communities without a healthy food system."[7] In 2008, the John D. and Catherine T. MacArthur Foundation awarded Allen one of its "genius" grants in honor of his work.

And in Detroit itself there is Earthworks Urban Farm, a network of parcels owned by the local Capuchins, the Roman Catholic order of friars who, among other things, run a soup kitchen for people in need.[8] Earthworks occupies several different parcels near the monastery, which itself is the anchor of a Detroit eastside neighborhood dotted with houses, vacant lots, and light industry. The monastery is the same one where Solanus Casey, a Capuchin friar now in line for canonization by the Roman Catholic Church, fed Detroit's poor and needy for two generations. Anyone who doubts the cooks and volunteers at food banks and soup kitchens know their business need only attend the Capuchin's annual Harvest Dinner. The charity event draws urban activists of all stripes (the speaker at the 2009 dinner was the famous Grace Lee Boggs, ninety-five years old and sitting in her wheelchair but an impassioned speaker all the same). The buffet line at the 2009 dinner included, among much else, a ratatouille, a

Fresh food grows in Chicago just off busy Michigan Avenue. (Author photo)

vegetarian curry, and a homemade crumble cake with berries flambé drizzled on top.

The Capuchins first planted Earthworks Urban Farm near their soup kitchen in 1997, and by 2009 the office of Patrick Crouch, the manager, was a maze of spreadsheets keeping track of dozens of crops planted on a complex rotation: tomatoes, strawberries, pumpkins, kale, cilantro, carrots, Swiss chard, basil, sunflowers, eggplant, squash, beans, cabbage, peas, peppers, garlic. Crouch and his staff and the legions of volunteers grow so many kinds of leafy greens that he calls the frequent tours he conducts for visitors "a walking salad bar." He says, "I'm stuffing it in their face saying, 'Try this! Try this!'" With his expansive red beard and his technical savvy about crops, Crouch may seem like a man born to the soil. But he grew up in Maryland and earned a fine arts degree before he found his calling in organic agriculture and food justice.

Earthworks also has a beekeeper, Stacey Malasky, and in 2008, the farm produced about nine hundred pounds of honey, a total which it hoped to exceed

Earthworks Urban Farm in Detroit remains a national model of nonprofit urban farming. (Author photo)

during the 2009 season. Earthworks operates a Growing Healthy Kids program, in which children barely as tall as some of the plants learn where their food comes from. In 2004, Earthworks added a 1,300-square-foot greenhouse that today produces more than one hundred thousand vegetable seedlings each year for gardens all over Detroit, Highland Park, and Hamtramck in the nonprofit Garden Resource Program Collaborative.

Hundreds of volunteers help with the harvest each year, picking berries and sampling the grape tomatoes right off the vine. Earthworks' range of prepared products, sold for promotional purposes and to support the Capuchins' mission, now include honey, jams, and Earthworks' own beeswax hand balm.

Las Parcelas, Growing Power, and Earthworks stand out as exceptional examples of urban farming, but there are thousands of other community gardens across America. And there are many organizations, like Philadelphia Green and the Detroit Agricultural Network, that provide everything from seeds and soil testing to tools and technical advice to would-be urban farmers. In a bid to be self-sustaining, by 2009 the nonprofit Detroit Agricultural Network was growing 150,000 organic transplants each year. The network, a group of collaborative organizations, has been working hard to develop its own seeds, mostly open pollinated varieties, and it's now producing most of its own tomato seed and bean seed. The network learned early on that while it might distribute the best resources, if people didn't know how to use them, the opportunity would pass them by. So the network conducts a lot of education—outdoors, hands-in-the-dirt variety. For example, an Urban Roots program consists of forty-five-hour, nine-week classes for gardeners.

With so much nourishment, the gardening community movement in Detroit has been flourishing. By the 2009 season, the Garden Resource Network was helping 517 family gardens, forty-six school gardens, and 244 community gardens. The return rate—those who come back season after season—was running at 82 percent. How much food do Detroit gardeners grow? Ashley Atkinson, the head of farming activities for the Greening of Detroit organization and the Ag Network, told a gathering I attended that during the 2009 season, community gardeners in the city would grow 330,000 pounds of food. Growers either consume that food themselves or give it away to neighbors, but that production level could command, in theory, a market value of around a half-million dollars.[9] Farming inside Detroit has sprouted from almost nothing in the year 2000 to a widespread and significant phenomenon by decade's end.

Many of the farm plots in Detroit are quite small, patches little bigger than a backyard. But those tiny plots add up. Driving around the city, one sees fenced gardens with rows of vegetables or small greenhouses or beehives at least every few blocks. Artwork and signs bearing heroic slogans (for example, "Hope Takes Root") adorn many of these gardens.

On Detroit's east side, not far from City Airport, a young man named William Gardner started his Edgeton Community Garden in 2009 on four vacant lots. He grows a wide variety of plants—lettuce, broccoli, peppers, potatoes, raspberries, carrots, beets, okra, beans, Swiss chard, and more. I met him one Saturday morning in the summer of 2009 at Eastern Market, where he and other city growers were selling produce at the Grown in Detroit stand. Gardner told me he'd come to the stand twice so far that season, and that he tried to bring about thirty dollars worth of food from his garden each time. That's the only cash his garden brings in, since he encourages his neighbors to come and pick their own food. "It's not really a business," he told me. "Mainly the produce is for the neighbors and they come and pick, so it's pretty cool." Another of Gardner's

The building blocks of a local food system: Detroit's Eastern Market on a busy Saturday morning. (Author photo)

motives, held in common with community gardeners everywhere, is restoring his own piece of the urban fabric. "It beautifies the neighborhood," Gardner said. His neighbors "tell me how nice it looks. The empty space, it's just been sitting there, and I try to make a landmark for the neighborhood that they can enjoy."

All this growing may do something for property values, too. A New York University study published in 2006 reported that opening a community garden in New York City produced a statistically significant positive impact on residential property values within a thousand feet of the garden.[10] The positive impact got bigger over time. This study found that higher quality gardens delivered the biggest boost to property values, and that gardens in the poorest urban neighborhoods produced the greatest results. Researchers Vicki Been and Ioan Voicu estimated that the city's gross tax benefit generated by all community gardens over a twenty-year period came to about $563 million— hardly small change! When any city subsidies were subtracted, community gardens still produced property value benefits of more than $750,000 per garden.

Many farmers might nod in agreement with those findings, but most growers are not in community gardening with economics in mind. Community bonding remains a key goal of virtually all the urban gardeners in America. Even the simplest community garden gets planted with the kernel of a hope that neighbors will gather together in a common, healthy, invigorating activity. Urban agriculture is an act of faith in a sea of despair.

While it's easy to rhapsodize about community gardening and the dedicated farmers who make it happen, if we're to use urban agriculture to remedy a place like Detroit, we also need to take a sober look at the obstacles that confront urban farming. Those obstacles are many, and they're serious.

WEEDS IN THE URBAN GARDEN

As I write these pages, Detroit still lacks any zoning classification for urban farming, a deficit it shares with many other cites. From a city planner's perspective, that makes community gardens, if not illegal, at least a nonconforming land use subject to ticketing and fines. The city doesn't actually ticket farmers, as everyone recognizes the benefits of community gardens. But as one city staffer told me, it's long past time for city codes to recognize the reality of urban agriculture.

In a place like Detroit with so much vacant land and so little to fill it, community growers face virtually no threat of city officials making trouble for them, but in cities with a more active real estate market, where available sites can be worth a lot of money, urban farmers do find themselves on the receiving end of official wrath, and vice versa. In New York City in the late 1990s, then-mayor Rudolph Giuliani enraged urban farmers by proposing to destroy more than a hundred community gardens planted on city-owned lots to build new housing. New York certainly needs more housing, but the gardens, like those we've looked at in Philadelphia, Detroit, and Milwaukee, had become the centers of the communities, providing not only fresh produce but also a rallying point for residents. Confronted by protesters, Giuliani taunted that they were stuck in the era of communism.[11] Only a last-minute deal saved many of the gardens: benefactors led by celebrity Bette Midler purchased more than a hundred of the city-owned lots to keep them in the hands of community growers. But the long-term conflict did not end. The battle between growers and developers in New York has been marked by lawsuits, protest, and acrimony.

Even in Detroit, city officials, ever optimistic about repopulating the depleted neighborhoods, tell activists like Paul Bairly, the head of tree planting for the nonprofit Greening of Detroit, that any plantings he conducts should be "temporary" in nature.[12] Well, yes, some future development might come along that would require gardeners to move aside for the greater good, just as landmark old buildings fall to make way for promised new projects (which, of course, often never get built). One expert perhaps captured the dilemma best when he called community gardens a "long-term temporary use."[13] Community gardens may be one of the saving graces for cities, but absent a strong commitment from authorities and solid legal backing, the gardens can disappear almost on a whim.

SOIL QUALITY

Soils in cities have seen a lot of hard use the past couple of centuries. We've compacted them under roads and buildings, buried debris from old structures, created a legacy of lead-based fuels and other contaminants. The question many skeptics raise about urban agriculture is whether that soil today is safe enough to grow crops for human food. Joan Nassauer, University of Michigan professor of landscape architecture, believes some of our hopes for community gardening in cities are bound to be disappointed.

I think that we have to be cautious about our aspirations for what can be achieved on vacant property with urban agriculture. My first and primary caution has to do with human health and the landscape legacies of properties that have been fully functioning in a tight street grid during decades when lead-based fuels were used. A lot of these properties have had demolitions of the existing structures that couldn't be absolutely thorough in dealing with common contaminants like asbestos, say. There's a lot of variety. Often there has been cleanups and it's getting better and better and better, but even where you have a bona fide brownfield cleanup, the difference between intent and technology is something that we all need to be aware of. I think we just need to be very thoughtful about what I see as sometimes a romantic notion of returning urban land to agriculture.[14]

Groups that promote urban farming like Greening of Detroit and Earthworks Urban Farm understand these risks and help potential growers understand them. These nonprofit groups test the soil of any potential garden site and let the farmers know when it's a good idea to move elsewhere. Rebecca Salminen Witt, president of the Greening of Detroit, told me that testing proves most sites to be safe, even in Detroit. Occasionally a site proves too contaminated; in Detroit, those are mostly the old industrial sites. But most former residential lots are clean enough, Witt says.[15] Even so, many urban gardeners pick as many bits of glass and other debris out of their garden plots as weeds.

If the soil is contaminated, we possess a variety of techniques for dealing with it. Some growers avoid the problem entirely by importing new soil. In this scenario, gardeners construct raised beds, which are simply wood boxes into which gardeners put new dirt. (Nailing boards together to create the boxes for raised beds presents another great opportunity for a neighborhood work project.) Some growers combine raised beds with greenhouses, and a few employ hydroponics, although growing crops in water takes more technology and know-how. A lot of old factory sites get turned into urban farms through such techniques; growers use the space, but not the underlying soil.

Some growers sidestep the question of contamination entirely by growing crops not for food consumption but for industrial use. Sunflowers remain the plant of choice for many of these growers. The oil from the plants can be turned into fuel, and a field of sunflowers delights the eye. And sunflowers and many other plants help clean up soils through a process known as phytoremediation—a gradual removal of contaminants over time. But when it comes to phytoremediation, Nassauer again raises a cautionary hand.

Bioremediation, and the use of sunflowers is an example of that, is an idea that has such great romantic appeal, and it really does work for some contaminants sometimes, but even for the contaminants for which certain plants are good

A community garden in Detroit's Midtown district in which raised beds solved the problem of building atop a contaminated site. (Author photo)

Urban agriculture on Detroit's west side. (Author photo)

remediators, bioacculmulators, even where they're effective, an issue with phytoremediation is it's irregular. It doesn't uniformly clean anything, because plants are not uniform and sunflowers are not in any way a solve-all solution. And I just think all of us in cities, especially where you have a legacy of demolitions and a long-time legacy of lead-based fuels, I just think we really need to be heads up about that. So my fear is that as community groups and NGOs and local governments get involved in thinking about alternative uses of land, we aren't sufficiently cautious about unintended effects of past contamination. The object lesson for all of us should be lead-based paint, which seemed like not that big a deal until fifteen years ago until lead levels in kids started to be measured, and we changed the way we make our paint. But with demolitions it's not quite as easy to just change the past because these demos hold the past in place.[16]

Community gardeners run to the idealistic, which helps motivate them to accomplish a huge amount of good in cities. But the cautions of Nassauer and other doubters about urban farming should not be brushed aside. The policy agenda remains clear: We need to test our soil on a lot-by-lot basis before we farm, and we need to conduct more research on how plants absorb contaminants in the soil and which plants work best in an urban setting. Cities, foundations, universities, and corporations all need to recognize the importance of these tasks and make them a primary focus of study and action.

LACK OF FARMERS

A Michigan farmer named Rob Ruhlig farms about a thousand acres in rural Monroe County south of Detroit down near the Ohio line. His farm is a family enterprise going back decades. When Ruhlig was in high school, he enlisted several of his friends to work with him in his family's fields. It proved instructive. The *best* worker, he told me on the day I visited his farm, lasted no more than two weeks. Most of his friends walked out on him much sooner.[17]

Farming is hard work. Full-time field work is hot, dirty, low-paid, and ranks far down the scale of what society considers a prestigious job. Even running the business end of a working farm—trucking the produce to market and lining up wholesale buyers and the like—requires a year-round commitment to long hours, thin profit margins, and not enough sleep.

"Let's have a look at what the industry is like," suggests Robin Boyle, Wayne State University professor of urban planning. "Low skilled, low income, temporary, dangerous. Why would a young black kid want to do that? It's very, very hard work for very low return on a piece of dirt."[18]

Community gardeners, being mostly volunteers, don't mind putting in a few hours a week or a month in a small urban patch. Tellingly, almost all of the urban gardens I see driving around Detroit have no one working in them except for some weekend and evening hours.

The problem of finding people to grow the crops looms large if urban farming is to achieve anywhere near its potential. And that means dealing with negative stereotypes of farming as a dull, rural activity best left to middle-aged or older folks—that's it's anything but "cool." Do young people really want to put down their iPhones to grow vegetables? Perhaps not. But someone will have to work down on the farm if we want our food system to morph into something much more locally based than it is now.

BIG VERSUS SMALL

A Detroit businessman named John Hantz created a splash in the spring of 2009 when he proposed building Detroit's first large commercial farm in the city, using hundreds or even thousands of vacant and abandoned parcels.[19] Hantz envisioned growing a wide variety of products—anything from lettuce and rhubarb to Christmas trees and holly bushes—and selling it wholesale to big customers like universities, hospitals, and retail markets. To generate income, Hantz would rent out part of his land for wind turbines; he would also operate a petting zoo and a riding stable for kids, and try to encourage families and agricultural tourists to visit.

Does that sound like a plan for creating value and for filling up some of Detroit's empty spaces? To Hantz it did. A resident of Detroit's Indian Village district, Hantz told me he used to marvel at all the pheasants he saw on his daily drive through largely abandoned neighborhoods toward the Lodge Freeway, which he took to his office in Southfield. So much vacant land, he mused. Why not fill it up with something useful?

Thus was born his idea for Hantz Farms, for which he hired Michael Score, a Michigan State University agricultural educator and counselor, to oversee. The business model envisions persuading the city of Detroit to hand over to Hantz a lot of the vacant land acquired through tax foreclosure, at a price of little or nothing. Actually, Hantz projected a total cost of three thousand dollars per acre, including legal expenses and the like, which works out to under three hundred dollars per vacant residential lot, which is pretty small potatoes even in a city with such poor real estate values as Detroit. In return for getting some of the city's vacant land—anywhere from several hundred to several thousand vacant parcels were mentioned—Hantz would invest his own money—perhaps one million dollars—in getting the farm up and running. He hoped to hit a hundred thousand dollars in revenue pretty quickly, within a year or two, and go on from there. He'd hire Detroit residents to work the farm, and do his best to act as a good neighbor to residents near the farm.

But if Hantz hoped that Detroit's many community gardeners would welcome his plan and become his fast friends, he quickly learned that many of them saw themselves as his natural enemies. The motives that underlie community gardening in cities today—social justice, community building, and healing a wounded environment—clash, at least in the minds of the community gardeners, with the notion of big corporate farming. Think about it: Many of these urban farmers feel betrayed by corporations for many reasons—because the banks and big business redlined Detroit and other cities, or because of the horror stories they hear about the way corporate farmers treat livestock, or because of the intensive use of pesticides and other chemicals corporate farmers use to make huge single-crop farms profitable. The community gardeners want no part of any of that. Many feel satisfaction and pride through gardening precisely because their gardens exist off the grid and far from the corporate world. Many urban farmers distrust Big Agriculture the same way they distrust Big Oil and Big Money.

This blend of community activism, social ideals, and distrust of big business turns most community farmers into instant critics of people like John Hantz and of his plan for large-scale commercial farming. Patrick Crouch, the manager of the nonprofit Earthworks Urban Farm in Detroit, questioned whether commercial farms spread over large plots of land were the best option for Detroit. "I see that as community annihilation and not community development," he said.[20]

Rebecca Salminen Witt of the Greening of Detroit agrees. She told me that small community plots do more good for Detroiters, helping knit communities together. She would like to see community farms top out at no more than about three acres. Proposals like Hantz Farms, she said, provide a false hope of solving Detroit's problem of widespread abandonment. "Folks are hoping for, wishing for, looking for a silver bullet to the vast expanses of vacant space that we see in the city," Witt said. "And because of that, they want to say, 'Great, we'll just plunk a couple of hundred-acre growing operations here and there.'"[21]

Kami Pothukuchi, an associate professor of urban planning at Wayne State University and the founder of the SEED Wayne program to promote sustainable food systems, offers a nuanced view of this question of big versus small. "I don't think there's opposition to profit or making money out of it," she told me. "It's the large commercial scale and what that might entail and the possible nuisances it might produce." Those nuisances might include dust, noise from farm machinery, and the destruction of the city's traditional urban fabric. Then, too, she added, commercial farmers typically aim for a single bottom line—the profit motive—instead of the multiple bottom lines that motivate nonprofit community farmers, including better health and nutrition for residents, and the building of neighborhood solidarity.[22]

Matt Allen, a spokesman for Hantz's farm project, patiently assured everyone that Hantz Farms would not compete with the community gardeners, that Detroit has land enough for growers big and small, and that Hantz Farms didn't plan a mono-crop operation like those cornfields in Iowa but something much like agriculture as it's already practiced in Michigan—many different crops, perhaps dozens in all, with room set aside for neighbors to come in and plant their own little vegetable patches.[23]

So far, though, whatever decision municipal leaders make on the Hantz Farms proposal, the idea hasn't won over the community gardeners. Make no mistake: Community voices raised against proposals like John Hantz's erect no small roadblock. Detroit city officials and staffers have long listened to such voices on issues large and small. City council member JoAnn Watson once delighted her supporters but horrified real estate professionals by suggesting that all of the land that the city owned through tax foreclosure and other means be kept in perpetuity by the city in a land trust.[24] That is, developers would be permitted to rent the space from the city and build projects on the land, but the city would still own the land and the city would reap any increase in the value of the land. Critics quickly pointed out that the idea would chill, if not kill, new development, because developers want the opportunity to profit fully from their investment, something Watson's idea would deny them. Watson's proposal died, but the episode revealed the city's underlying distrust of, and perhaps ignorance of, the workings of everyday capitalism.

As of early 2010, city leaders were still studying the proposal, and Hantz and Score were still trying to sell them on his plan and hoping to plant some demonstration crops on land they had purchased on the city's east side. But the conflict is real. Community distrust of commercial farming, and the perception that big farming would threaten rather than help ordinary Detroit families, presents at least as serious an obstacle to Hantz Farms and similar proposals as soil quality and other technical challenges.

THE VASTNESS OF THE VACANCY

Whatever the many benefits of community gardening and however enthused we grow over urban agriculture, the sheer size of Detroit's empty spaces is likely to absorb community growers as Lake Michigan absorbs a passing shower. Consider a few facts. If the Greening of Detroit people are correct, in 2009 Detroit enjoyed some eight hundred community gardens. The largest was a couple of acres. As I've said, most of the community gardens remain quite small by farming standards, many measuring no more than perhaps forty by forty feet, an area that translates into less than 5 percent of an acre. I've seen many community gardens in Detroit that size and smaller.

If we add the land area of all of Detroit's community gardens together, a good estimate of the total would be perhaps five hundred acres on the high side, or roughly one square mile. (A square mile equals 640 acres.) Yet Detroit, as we know, contains nearly forty square miles of vacancy, an area roughly the size of Boston or San Francisco. So urban farming, as positive a force as many of us believe it to be, won't solve our vacancy problem in Detroit, unless we get serious about allowing businessmen like John Hantz, or a Detroit drug treatment group called SHAR that has proposed a similar but nonprofit version called RecoveryPark, to farm hundreds of acres at a time. Absent large commercial farms, what do we do with the other 98.6 percent of Detroit's empty land?

Any discussion of large-scale farming in Detroit leads inevitably to our next topic: money.

DOLLARS AND SENSE

Revenue from the urban farms that do exist in Detroit is slowly increasing. A coalition of several nonprofit farming groups sells locally grown food at farmers markets under a Grown in Detroit label. Ashley Atkinson of the Detroit Agricultural Network told an audience in 2009 that the Grown in Detroit label would sell about sixteen thousand dollars' worth of produce that year—up from a mere eight hundred dollars five years earlier.[25] One also hears other success stories: a grower in the Latino neighborhood of southwest Detroit making salsa for sale to Mexican restaurants, or a local teacher who earns a thousand dollars a month in the summer selling produce from his Detroit garden plot. All these sales represent the first faint stirrings of a local farming economy in Detroit.

At this writing, a handful of efforts were under way to scale up Detroit's nascent agriculture into something that would attract investors and produce economic returns as well as the nutritional and other intangible benefits. The Greening of Detroit was planning to operate a 2.5-acre plot near Eastern Market in the spring of 2010 to demonstrate farming techniques and to help would-be farm entrepreneurs learn to market their products. A nationally known New York City activist, Majora Carter, visited Detroit in December 2009 to pitch her idea for a nationwide worker-owned urban agriculture cooperative with Detroit as the pilot city. The Kresge Foundation and other funders were expressing tentative interest in Carter's proposal. A MacArthur "genius" grant honoree for her work in the South Bronx, Carter told me she would like to see urban agriculture scale up very quickly to profit-making status. That would help empower poor people in our cities who otherwise might lack any resources for self-help.[26]

Then, too, Kami Pothukuchi of Wayne State University helped debut a new farmers market on WSU's campus in 2009. The market, on Cass north of Warren, operated on twenty-five selling days during the season, and Pothukuchi estimated that about a thousand shoppers stopped by each day. The growers who participated did not reveal how much money they made, but if a thousand shoppers spent, say, an average of four dollars on each of these shopping days, the market would have seen a hundred thousand dollars in total sales. Whether anyone made any profit once expenses were deducted is another matter, of course.

These efforts are intriguing. But, as I've said, community growers aren't in it for the money. Even the best urban farms, the ones that are nationally recognized, such as Earthworks in Detroit, Growing Power in Milwaukee, and Las Parcelas in Philadelphia, are not run as profit-making businesses. They operate with support from foundations or city subsidies and, of course, with lots and lots of volunteer labor. They're wonderful institutions doing enormous good in their cities. But they're not *businesses*.

A business is an activity that brings in enough revenue to attract investors and entrepreneurs, one that will pay its workers a living wage adequate to support them and their families. How much revenue does a good business have to bring in? The median household income in the United States is about $45,000. If a farm running as a business wanted to employ ten workers at that level of income—marketers and accountants and machine operators and truck drivers— it would have to generate about a half-million dollars a year in revenue just to pay these workers. Not to mention the additional cost of field hands and tractors and delivery trucks and legal help and insurance policies and everything else a farm business requires.

The utopian ideal envisioned by many community gardeners of a city feeding itself with nonprofit volunteer farms in every neighborhood may, in fact, come true. Striving for social justice in the form of locally grown food motivates powerfully. But if we expect urban agriculture to contribute to the *economic* as well as the *nutritional* health of a city, we need to start thinking about making it a paying game.

And that brings us to our final obstacle.

THE LACK OF A LOCAL FOOD ECONOMY

Try this experiment: Go to your refrigerator or pantry and read the labels on your food and see where it comes from. If you're like me and 99 percent of other Americans, your food comes from pretty far away. Now and then, I eat a bowl of oatmeal for breakfast. The box of oatmeal comes from Ireland, the raisins I mix in come from California, my glass of orange juice from Florida. Various researchers have offered estimates on how far on average our food travels to our plates, with around 1,500 miles a commonly quoted number. The author and environmentalist Bill McKibben captures this reality in a pithy phrase. Our food, he says, comes marinated in oil—crude oil.[27]

Nor is that surprising given how our far-flung food economy operates. To produce the rising profits that keep Wall Street happy, agribusinesses relentlessly squeeze out costs. That translates into running huge crop and animal lots, paying low wages to migrant farm workers, using a maximum of preservatives, and placing a premium on marketing and packaging. Small, local growers hardly stand a chance.

Whatever the nutritional implications, our nonlocal food system takes an economic toll on a community like Detroit. Dan Carmody, the president of the nonprofit Eastern Market Corporation in Detroit, ventures that we now get no more than 2 percent of our food from local sources. If we could boost that to even 5 to 10 percent, the economic impact—in wages paid to farm workers, in the profits earned by local food processing plants, in the additional tax revenues garnered by local and state governments—would be staggering.

To help us understand the implications of local food system, we turn to Mike Hamm, C. S. Mott Professor of Sustainable Agriculture at Michigan State University, who is one of the nation's experts on urban farming and its effects on the food system.[28] Hamm estimates that the average person in the United States needs about 1,200 pounds of food a year, not counting coffee, tea, alcohol, soft drinks, and added sugar and fats. So the United States, with its population of three hundred million, needs to produce or import about 360 billion pounds of food a year to feed its people. We have about ten million people in Michigan, so we need about twelve billion pounds of good food a year to feed the state. And the city of Detroit, with its population of around 900,000, needs about 1.08 billion pounds of food each year. We need a lot of food.

Hamm says that 35 percent of the fresh fruits and vegetables that we eat every day in the United States comes from nondomestic sources. That percentage increases every year, partly because of our taste for exotics but significantly because we continue to lose farmland in the United States to new development. Of what we produce domestically, about 86 percent of that is produced on threatened land, that is, land that's under threat of development. About 60 percent of our dairy products come from land threatened by development. California produces about 50 percent of the domestic produce grown in the United States, and California is threatened by continuing water shortages. Most of the produce grown in California is irrigated with snowmelt that comes out of the mountains in the spring and summer. Climate change scenarios predict we could lose as much as 70 percent of that snowpack runoff over next thirty to fifty years. About eight hundred thousand acres of once-arable land in California's Central Valley are no longer under production because of drought. "We probably will not be able to source the food that we are today from the same places to the same extent we do today," Hamm warns. "And we're going to have more people. And if everybody woke up tomorrow and starting eating all the fruits and veggies they should, we're about thirteen million acres short of production for all of us to eat our recommended daily requirement of fresh fruits and vegetables. That's two or three Californias."

Urban farms currently fill a just a tiny portion of our food needs. As we've seen, the Greening of Detroit estimates that, as of 2009, Detroit's urban gardeners grow about 330,000 pounds of food a year. Using Hamm's estimate of 1,200 pounds per person per year, the output of Detroit's urban gardeners could feed only about 275 people a year, out of a city of 800,000 to 900,000. "We need a lot of food," Hamm says.

> A lot of people that I work with are really focused on very small-scale agriculture, which is a great thing, and the question is, how many of those small agricultures does it take to generate 360 billion pounds of food? And the answer is, quite a bit. We could go on the way that we're going, which is to continue to increase the share of our food that comes from nondomestic sources. I'm not either an advocate or somebody who is against global trade by any stretch of the imagination. But I think one of the questions we have to ask ourselves is, have we tipped the scale too far? Have we gone so far down the road of sourcing our food supply that we're in danger of losing our food supply down the road?

At this point, a lot of people object that they don't want to give up their city jobs to become farmers or give up imported coffee, bananas, mangos, and many other items we enjoy. No one suggests that they do. Detroiters couldn't possibly stop importing food from California and Mexico and other faraway places.

We'd starve. But we can understand the trend and make some incremental adjustments. "Right now in most parts of the United States today, we have a food system that is distinctly not locally integrated," Hamm says. "We have basically destroyed the local production of almost anything that we consume on a regular basis and gotten it from more distant domestic sources and from nondomestic sources. We need to relocalize to the extent possible. If we can get it from local sources, let's do it."

One of Hamm's graduate students recently examined how much food Detroiters potentially could produce on city farms. Using city land records, the student found about 44,000 vacant publicly owned parcels of land—vacant lots. That equated to about 4,800 acres of land, which if combined would translate into a parcel about one mile wide and eight miles long. Then Hamm's student asked how much food we could produce on that land if we used certain techniques, such as greenhouses, to extend the growing season. The study found that on 3,600 acres Detroiters could produce 76 percent of the vegetables and 42 percent of the fruit needed for a healthy diet for a million people. That amount of production could employ thousands of people and result in millions of dollars of sales. "The option is there to think about producing significant amounts of food in the city," Hamm says. "This need not be a marginal activity in a place like Detroit."

To skeptics who say it can't be done, consider the example of craft beers. Twenty years ago, almost anyone who drank beer in the United States had to settle for the mass-produced brands that, to many palates, were uninteresting at best. Then the small local brewers got in the game, brewing beers with more flavor, body, and character than the mass brands. They started at a very small level, but by word of mouth and some clever marketing, they grew. The Brewers Association, a trade group, estimates that craft brewing sales now account for 4 percent of all beer sales by volume and 6.3 percent by dollars, and in some parts of the marketplace, the numbers are even higher.[29]

Let's also consider, at some length, the example of Susan Schmidt, director of food service and catering at the Henry Ford, the vast collection of Americana in Dearborn, Michigan, that includes both the Henry Ford Museum and Greenfield Village. Sporting four restaurants and a robust wedding-and-catering trade, the Henry Ford spends around two million dollars a year on food supplies. When

Schmidt took over her job several years ago, the institution was still buying like most other big organizations, getting lettuce and beans from California or Texas or from wherever their national distributors shipped it. Then Schmidt had her awakening.

The site of her epiphany was the historic Eagle Tavern, one of the restaurants at the Henry Ford. The tavern operates as living history, its servers dressed in period costumes and its chefs cooking recipes out of the 1850s. So authentic is the tavern that servers' costumes are made without zippers, since the zipper wasn't invented until a later period. "We're doing all this great stuff," Schmidt told me, "but the ingredients that we were using to prepare these authentic recipes were coming from conventional sources and conventional distributors. So it occurred to me that if we wanted to make this even more authentic, the ingredients would have come from local farms and local sources because that's what happened then."[30]

Schmidt started out buying local fruits and vegetables, and then moved on to local cheese, meat, grains, and more. The annual holiday dinners at Eagle Tavern include a signature dish, the pork-and-apple pie, and Schmidt buys many hundreds of pounds of pork from a local farmer named Alvin Ernst. And the chestnuts roasted each year at holiday time? The Henry Ford buys thousands of pounds of chestnuts each year from a local growers' cooperative.

At harvest time, Schmidt told me, as much as 60 percent of the food served at the Henry Ford restaurants will be locally sourced. There will be less local food available, of course, during the off-season, but across a full year Schmidt estimates that she's sourcing 20 to 30 percent of all food from local producers. "If we're going to buy something," she told me, "our first filter is always, 'Can we get it from somebody local?' And a second filter would be, 'Can we get it from somebody in Michigan?'" She estimates that, in 2008, the Henry Ford spent about half a million dollars on locally sourced food.

Getting to that level took some doing, of course. When she started to think local, Schmidt had to search the Internet and talk to like-minded people about where to find what she needed. Gradually she evolved a network of farmers and wholesalers who could deliver what she wanted. And then she had to organize her kitchens all over again. "We had to train cooks how to cook again in some ways," Schmidt said. "Because it's different than when you open a bag and pour

Locally sourced food on the menu during the annual holiday dinner at Eagle Tavern at The Henry Ford in suburban Detroit. (Courtesy The Henry Ford)

Chef Nick Seccia, Executive Chef for the Henry Ford, picks vegetables and herbs in the gardens of Greenfield Village. (Courtesy The Henry Ford)

something out than if you get something that may still have a little dirt on the roots and you have to figure out what to do with real food." The fear that locally sourced food would be more expensive than buying from a corporate distributor proved unfounded. "We have been able to do what we do and still make our food-cost budget, which is at or below industry standards," Schmidt said.

Today, Schmidt preaches the gospel of local to anyone who will listen. "One of the reasons why it was important for us to do this was so that we could model it for other food businesses and institutions," she said. Schmidt has helped Wayne State University and other local schools become more locally sourced, and each year, urban planning associate professor Kami Pothukuchi sends some of her students to Schmidt for training in operating a sustainable local food business.

Perhaps the half-million dollars in locally sourced food used at the Henry Ford may not be much by the standards of the multi-billion-dollar local food economy. But that amount is growing, and it's a sign of what may one day be possible.

"It's kind of like, if there's a will, there's a way," Schmidt told me. "I like to say we took a giant leap of faith backwards."

Creating a more local food system won't be easy. If we hope to transform today's nonlocal food system in even a modest way, we'll need to offer a profit motive to draw in entrepreneurs and workers. We'll need to ramp up our distribution networks and vastly expand the amount of acreage under cultivation. Local institutions such as universities and hospitals will need to follow the Henry Ford's example and work out more complex arrangements with local suppliers instead of simply ordering processed food and megaquantities from single giant suppliers. The economics of urban farming, now an afterthought, will demand attention.

There's an irony here. Neither small community gardeners nor giant agribusinesses seem capable of meeting in the middle, which is where the future of urban farming may lie. The nonprofit community-based gardens find it impossible to scale up to, say, fifty to five hundred acres of production, while the corporate farming operations cannot operate on anything less than prodigious scales. Eating local—fresh, nutritious food grown within a few miles of our homes—requires us to solve the riddle of that economic system.

ONE FARMER'S FIRST YEAR

In the spring of 2009, my wife and I joined about a dozen more Detroiters to plant a community garden in the city's West Village district. The garden is called Shipherd Greens, after one of the streets that runs past it. Our neighbors had first planted Shipherd Greens a couple of years before, and the narrow rectangular beds, perhaps three by eight feet, remained visible that April evening in the spring grass even after the long, cold winter. Our fellow growers comprised a mix of lifelong city dwellers and recent transplants from the suburbs, young and old, skilled at gardening and absolute beginners (I was firmly in the neophyte category).

Lisa Richter, the energetic outreach director for the nonprofit Earthworks Urban Farm, got us started. She provided the seedlings courtesy of Earthworks, and we divvied up the available plots, pulled the weeds, and set to planting. My wife and I that first day planted tomatoes, carrots, radishes, and beets. Others planted lettuce, garlic, collard greens, and scallions. The understanding was that the produce would be free to the neighborhood. A nearby resident who had pulled down an old brick wall donated the bricks, and we hauled armfuls of them across the street to line our planting beds to help keep the weeds at bay.

At that first planting, I knew next to nothing about raising vegetables. Aside from a few tomato plants my parents had raised in my teen years, the earliest in the growing cycle I had ever encountered veggies was the supermarket aisle, or perhaps at a stand at a farmers market. Now I read up on the two varieties of tomatoes I had planted (San Marzano, an Italian variety good for sauces, and Cherokee Purple). I visited Shipherd Greens a few times a month to weed our plot, mow the grass with a borrowed mower, and otherwise tidy up.

And, lo, the earth proved fruitful, even our much abused Detroit dirt, from which I picked bits of glass and other debris along with the weeds. Everything sprouted in amazing variety and abundance. Once, as we bicycled past on a weekend, my wife stopped and picked a green onion. Handing the thick, fibrous stalk to me, she told me to try it, so I bit off a chunk. Fresh from the earth, it was unlike any onion I had ever tasted—pungent, full of flavor, almost too intense to eat raw. We pulled up a head of lettuce for our salad that evening. Tomatoes

The Shipherd Greens garden in Detroit's West Village district. (Author photo)

were ripening by late July, and I was harvesting carrots (rather short and stubby but still tasty) in August.

As the first growing season grew to a close, I could hardly claim to be a farmer, even a citified version of one. I still had to ask the other gardeners which plant was which (they all look green, you know). I found that letting tomatoes hang too long on the vine means they'll drop off to rot on the ground and then have to be tossed on the compost pile. Yet, inept as I was, I had learned a few things—about the neighborhood, about growing vegetables, and about a possible future for our cities.

4

ROAD DIETS AND ROUNDABOUTS

A lot of dates have proved pivotal in Detroit's history. Cadillac arrived in 1701, and the city burned to ashes in 1805. Henry Ford offered five dollars a day to workers in 1914. The racial explosions of 1967 devastated the city and shredded its self-image as a peaceful haven where blacks and whites lived in harmony. But to explain where Detroit is today, no date looms as more important than 1939. That year, the General Motors Pavilion at the New York World's Fair presented the vision known as *Futurama*. A designer named Norman Bel Geddes created a huge model of a futuristic city circa 1960 notable for its many "magic motorways"—what we now know as freeways. Visitors lined up by the thousands to sit in elevated chairs that carried them around and above this great urban network of automobile traffic. In that future, General Motors told visitors, everyone would drive everywhere and be happy about it.

Like most futuristic visions, Futurama proved wide of the mark on some things. It imagined that vehicles and pedestrians would be kept on separate levels in our cities, instead of sharing the streets as we do. But in imagining the role the automobile would play in our future and the rise of the expressway as a dominant urban form, the GM exhibit of 1939 got it spot on. Ian Lockwood, a Florida-based urban planner for Glatting Jackson Kercher Anglin, Inc., has been working with the nonprofit Community Foundation for Southeast Michigan to undo the damage auto-based planning has done. Detroit in 1939, he told me, was poised on the cutting edge of just about everything, and it embraced Futurama more than any other place in North America. He said, "During this time, the United States was becoming a superpower and kind of defined itself around the car."[1]

It didn't happen immediately. World War II broke out, and the United States devoted its energies to defeating fascism for the next several years. But when things settled down after the war and American cities began expanding again, the freeway became the dominant expansion strategy. And, as Lockwood said, nobody did it with more gusto than Detroiters. The city killed off its light-rail streetcar lines (only now is Detroit struggling to rebuild even a single new light-rail line), and it rammed expressways through many still-vibrant city neighborhoods. The city's main arterial surface streets, such as Jefferson, Gratiot, and Woodward, became nine-lane highways linking downtown to the rapidly growing suburbs. And everyone thought it was a great idea. As it turned out, if you were designing a city to be easily abandoned, you couldn't have come up with a better plan than Detroit's.

"Unfortunately for Detroit, that was an ill-conceived vision," Lockwood told me. "It never succeeded anywhere it was tried. It tended to chop up the city, and the highways exported value from the city to the suburbs. And you can see that same pattern in Atlanta, Houston, everywhere this was done. Value left the city and went to the suburbs. And of course Detroit did it the most because it was the city of mosts, and did itself a great deal of harm."

UNDOING THE DAMAGE

From the perspective of 2010, as I write this book, I see that we can't do much about the expressways for now, other than patching the potholes. It's interesting to note, though, that other cities have begun to remove some of their freeways. Portland, Oregon, has removed one expressway from along its waterfront, and Seattle is talking about ripping out one of its freeways. Farther south, San Francisco has removed parts of *two* freeways. After that city removed its Embarcadero Freeway in 1991, real estate values in adjacent neighborhoods shot up. A new neighborhood began to thrive in the absence of the freeway that had cut that district off from the waterfront.

Could Detroit do without some of its expressways? The little spur known as I-375 adds almost nothing to the city's attractiveness or efficiency, running just a short distance along downtown's eastern edge, and it could go. So, perhaps, could the Lodge south of I-75. Remember, an expressway is supposed to carry motorists *to* the downtown, not slash its way *through* it.

But if, as I suspect, Detroit's expressways are off limits to reform for the foreseeable future, we can at least redesign the city's arterial "spoke" streets such as Jefferson, Michigan Avenue, and Grand River. This could significantly improve life for Detroit residents. To understand what I mean, first we'll need to look at those streets to see how they operate today.

Road Diets

When we think about vacancy in Detroit, we usually picture the urban prairie where homes and factories once stood. That's where the weeds grow tall and piles of tires spill into the street, and the ring-necked pheasants and red foxes roam. Numerous journalists and artists have documented that emptiness over the years. But we almost never focus on the wide-open spaces of our main streets. Making Woodward, Jefferson, Gratiot, and the other spoke streets nine lanes wide (three lanes for traffic in each direction, one in the middle for turning, and a lane along either curb for parking) may have made sense in the 1950s when the city boasted a population near two million people. But with Detroit's population less than half its 1950s-era peak, these main streets now are absurdly overbuilt for the amount of traffic they carry.

Scott Clein, an engineer with Detroit-based Giffels-Webster Engineers, is trying, like Ian Lockwood, to undo the damage of decades of auto-based urban planning. He showed me traffic studies of Michigan Avenue near downtown that suggest the street has far more capacity than it needs for the traffic it carries today.[2] That confirms my own informal observations, which anyone can duplicate by simply standing on a corner along East Jefferson Avenue or Gratiot or Grand River for several minutes in the middle of the day. You'll be amazed at how empty the city's major streets are much of the time. Even during rush hour, traffic heading downtown from suburbs like Grosse Pointe tends to be heavy but not continuous. It clumps up at red lights, but these thickets of vehicles can be widely separated from the next batch.

This excess capacity creates an opportunity to put our major streets on what reformers call a "road diet." Many of Detroit's neighborhoods are cut off from each other by these overly wide streets. Pedestrians, particularly seniors or parents with children in tow, find it all but impossible to cross one of these nine-line gulfs before the light changes. By narrowing the streets from three traffic lanes in each direction to two—by putting many of Detroit's streets on a road diet—the city could make it easier for pedestrians to cross. We could also

Overcapacity in Detroit: even during weekday rush hour, East Jefferson Avenue, one of Detroit's busiest and most important streets, is empty for big stretches. (Author photo)

make room for alternative transportation like bicycles. That, in turn, would make neighborhoods more walkable, and, I hope, more livable.

Motorists may not like it, but they'll get used to it in Detroit as they have in other cities such as Portland and Denver, where bike lanes and public transit have greatly improved the quality of life. Meanwhile, Ann Arbor and other cities have begun installing traffic-calming devices like slightly raised intersections and wider sidewalks to slow down speeding traffic.

Traffic Calming

A lot of cities around the world have invested in traffic roundabouts, which are not to be confused with traffic circles, although both are round. New Jersey is infamous for its traffic circles. Traffic circles are designed to sling-shot cars at relatively high speeds into and through the traffic, and the cars entering the circle have right-of-way over those already in it. With every driver trying

A road diet idea: put a landscaped median down the center of East Jefferson Avenue near Belle Isle, as suggested by students during a 2009 planning charrette. (Courtesy the Villages of Detroit)

Another road diet idea: run a trolley line up the center of East Jefferson Avenue, as students suggested during a 2009 planning charrette. (Courtesy the Villages of Detroit)

to dodge and weave through the melee, traffic circles are dangerous and problematic.

A roundabout is much smaller. It's simply a concrete island, often landscaped, that sits within the middle of an intersection around which traffic flows. The vehicles already in the roundabout enjoy right-of-way over those entering. As a driver approaches a roundabout, he or she yields to those already in it and then enters when a gap appears.

Roundabouts offer several advantages for traffic management. Cars aren't idling at red lights for significant time, and they're not accelerating (and burning more fossil fuel) when the light turns green. Since speeds at a roundabout are naturally slower, drivers pay better attention to pedestrians and bicyclists. Roundabouts are safer than traffic circles and even signalized intersections because, as with narrower streets and wider sidewalks, drivers aren't expecting to race through them as fast as possible. As a bonus, roundabouts don't require any electricity for signal lights because you can dispense with the traffic signals entirely. That means maintenance costs are very low, too.

Roundabouts are surprisingly pedestrian friendly. Lockwood and his firm have been designing roundabouts for school crossings and in tourist areas to help pedestrians cross safely. Traffic tends to slow to fifteen to twenty miles per hour at a roundabout so everyone tends to yield to any pedestrians. "And it's beautiful compared to signals," Lockwood told me. "You get rid of all that clutter that's up in the sky, get rid of the box, get rid of the electricity costs, and all the baggage. Signals have baggage. They have all the turn lanes and all that extra asphalt. Most drivers speed up when they see a stale green light or a yellow light. Nobody speeds up for a roundabout. They're there 24-7, they're not moving. You slow down, you go around it."

Detroit, as usual, is well behind in the game. In the suburbs north of Detroit, the Oakland County Road Commission is already installing several roundabouts to smooth out traffic flow in the rapidly growing area.[3] And roundabouts are much more common in other parts of the world than in America at this point. Lockwood and his colleague Dan Burden, who have studied Detroit's streets, suggest a roundabout for the juncture of East Jefferson and Grand Boulevard, one of the most important intersections in Detroit. It marks the entrance to Belle Isle Park, and it separates the upscale residential districts of Indian Village and

Traffic slows naturally but keeps flowing at a typical roundabout. Roundabouts also lend themselves to greater landscaping than signalized intersections. (Courtesy Glatting Jackson Kercher Anglin)

the Gold Coast to the east from the approaches to downtown to the west. So a roundabout at that point would do more than slow traffic at a difficult pedestrian crossing. It would serve as a symbolic gateway, marking the transition between key districts of the city. "It just completely changes the environment of the intersection," Lockwood told me. "So instead of this hostile, ugly, car-oriented, antipedestrian entrance to a very important place, you get this civically beautiful gesture that outperforms the signals in practically every measurable way."

Streets Are for Everyone

After years of study, Detroit's city council approved a nonmotorized transportation plan for the city in 2008. It was an important gesture; it signaled that the city would take seriously efforts to promote bicycle commuting and other ways of linking the city's many districts. The hard work of implementing the plan must now take place; streets must be painted with bike lanes as money allows, and new walking paths can be created once funding sources are identified. Numerous other details remain for the future, including how to train police and other safety workers in an environment that supports nonmotorized transportation options, and how to enforce compliance by motorists with new

Above: A typical signalized intersection. *Below:* Architectural rendering of the same intersection with a roundabout. (Courtesy Glatting Jackson Kercher Anglin)

rules of behavior. As of the fall of 2009, staffers from various city departments were meeting every few weeks to sort out ideas.

Many people who heard about the nonmotorized plan assumed it means simply adding bicycle lanes, but there's more to it. The concept recognizes that traffic engineers ought to consider the needs not just of cars and trucks but of pedestrians, too, as well as bicyclists, people who use wheelchairs, and anyone else not motoring along in a car. Everything from the timing of traffic signals to the width of intersections comes into play. If city traffic engineers and heavy-footed suburban commuters say it can't be done, we can simply point to places where Detroit has already made such changes. Getting ready to host Super Bowl XL in 2006, the city created landscaped medians in three downtown streets—Washington Boulevard, Broadway, and Gratiot. It widened the sidewalks on Woodward Avenue, eliminating a traffic lane in each direction. And it created Campus Martius Park in the middle of downtown, forcing traffic on Woodward Avenue to slow down to navigate around it—in effect, creating a modified roundabout, albeit one with signals. All these changes slowed the flow of auto traffic, but the drivers got used to it, and we didn't see a big increase in either accidents or delays.

Author Tom Vanderbilt, in his valuable study *Traffic: Why We Drive the Way We Do*, points out that traffic engineers typically envision a safe road as an open road, with wide neutral zones bordering the street and few if any trees and other "obstacles" along the side of the road for drivers to crash into.[4] But statistically speaking, that wide-open, obstacle-free design tends to create *more* accidents, not fewer. Drivers freed from any environment restraints press the accelerator harder and pay less attention to crosswalks and incoming traffic from side streets. Older-style streets, narrower and lined with trees and bordered by sidewalks, see fewer accidents, at least fewer serious ones, because drivers learn to slow down and pay attention. Things like trees along the roadside, which many traffic engineers viewed as hazards, turn out to calm traffic and make it safer. As Vanderbilt writes, "The hazards *were* the safety device."[5]

Greenways

The suggestion to narrow Detroit's main streets and paint them with bicycle lanes is part of a broader effort to create "greenways" throughout Metro

If busy midtown Manhattan can handle a well-developed network of bicycle lanes and electronic signals, why can't Detroit? (Author photo)

Detroit. An outgrowth of the old rails-to-trails movement to convert unused railroad tracks to bike and walking paths, the greenways movement is aimed at connecting neighborhoods with parks, trails and other nonautomotive links. The Community Foundation for Southeast Michigan already has committed about twenty-five million dollars to creating greenways. As I write this, about a hundred miles of new greenways are in some stage of planning, construction, or completion in Metro Detroit.

Detroit's new RiverWalk is the city's most famous greenway. The Dequindre Cut also opened in 2009, a 1.3-mile paved trail linking the Detroit River with the Eastern Market district. The Conner Creek Greenway, also a paved pathway, parallels Conner Avenue on Detroit's east side for about three miles today; the goal is to have it run from the city's northern border at 8 Mile Road to the Detroit River. A Midtown Loop greenway path is under construction in the city's university and cultural district. Lesser paths continue to take shape around

Metro Detroit. The goal now is to knit them into a network that ties the region's many neighborhoods together.

Like anything else, greenways and traffic roundabouts and wider sidewalks and bicycle lanes cost money and require engineering, and they must be coordinated with any other revitalization efforts that are going on in any given district. But compared to building or maintaining nine-lane roads that sit empty much of the day, creating and maintaining nonmotorized transportation systems is a *lot* cheaper. And they do more good *for the people living in a city* than commuter highways that only speed drivers to distant communities. If Detroit can get honest about its population loss and stop dreaming about returning to a city of two million, if it can trim capacity from a road system that makes sense only if that implausible dream of a population rebound were to somehow come true, if it can do those things, then Detroit might discover a whole lot of relatively simple ideas to redesign its streets that would pay off big time.

The payoff would be a viable city for the rest of the twenty-first century.

HEALING A WOUNDED LANDSCAPE

Back in the mid-1990s, landscape architect Joan Nassauer accepted an invitation to see if she could help an ailing shopping center in St. Paul, Minnesota. At the time, Nassauer ran a design lab at the University of Minnesota; her interest, then and now, is restoring a more natural ecology to urban spaces. Perhaps when the local leaders invited her to take a look, they expected a more conventional solution—add some shrubbery here, or build a berm there, that sort of thing. Instead she gave them a fairly radical solution that, from today's perspective, helps us think about cities in a whole new way. "It was quite obvious that something was wrong here ecologically," Nassauer said of her early visits to the shopping center.[1] The big clue was that the elevation of the center was about a dozen feet lower than the ordinary high water level of Phalen Lake, a major body of water located upstream of the shopping center. Since water flows downhill, the land downstream of it tended to get wet. Build a shopping center on a wetland, and what do you get? Flooded basements. It was a chronic problem for the retail center.

Those wet basements provided one reason why the center didn't have very good success renting retail space. Then, too, a neighborhood group that had been meeting for a couple of years was concerned that the shopping center was a high-crime site. "And so somehow there's a vicious cycle," Nassauer told me. "The stores aren't doing so well, the rents are low, it attracts stores that don't do so well, the building isn't doing so well, and that lack of a demeanor of success tends to allow other social situations like crime to have a space."

Nassauer found an old map that showed a wetland located where the shopping center now sat. That helped explain why pavement in the parking lot there cracked. Nassauer told me, "The funniest thing was, almost always, except in the middle of winter, there'd be a pair of mallards paddling around in these puddles. *They* knew what it was." Some of the oldest residents of the neighborhood could remember going fishing in a small lake that had existed there before the site had been filled in.

Based on what they had learned, Nassauer and her colleagues and students came up with one outrageous suggestion: Rip out the shopping center and re-create a wetland park. "At first it was a shocking idea," she said. However, in part because people were looking for solutions to the problem of crime in the shopping center, and in part because wetlands deliver a lot of ecological benefits—they serve as natural holding tanks for rainwater so sewers don't overflow, and of course they create an attractive natural landscape—the city of St. Paul moved ahead with relocating commercial development to a nearby arterial street and tearing down the old shopping center to make way for a wetland park.

Once the Phalen Wetland Park project had been completed, its success was measured in more than rainwater retention. Not far from the old shopping center site, and providing one of the motivations for the project, ran a line of low-income subsidized housing. Once the city created the new wetland, those low-income housing units suddenly looked better (Think: instant waterfront views). And the city promoted a new project of higher-end, market-rate housing even closer to the new wetland. A loser of a strip mall had become a winning waterfront residential district.

The wetland park became almost too successful. Much of the new residential development came in the form of small cul-de-sacs arranged around the wetland. The effect, Nassauer says, was to compromise the original purpose of the project; a public amenity was fast becoming a private one. But those were complaints of success, not failure. The Phalen Wetland Park project created a new center for the community and dramatically increased local biodiversity. And the city and the taxpayers saved money because they didn't have to build as many pipes and pumping stations and the like because the volume of stormwater going into the sewers decreased dramatically.

Here's a thought: What if Detroit had decided, even ten years ago with the technology then at hand, to use not the heavily engineered, big-pipe system to deal with stormwater overflows, and instead used some of these softer solutions to keep rainwater in a natural setting within each neighborhood? How much money would the financially strapped city have saved over the years? "I don't even want to guesstimate, but I'm sure it would be a very big number," Nassauer told me.

The story of Phalen Wetland Park illustrates an important point that Detroit and other distressed cities can learn from. The movement from a natural environment to an asphalt-and-concrete cityscape doesn't have to go only in one direction. The progression can happen in reverse, too, and, when it does, a city can reap real benefits measured in property values and quality of life. Nor is Phalen Park an isolated case. Once you start to look for these natural solutions to urban problems, you can find examples all over the world.

PRISTINE STREAM

From the Middle Ages onward, the city of Seoul, South Korea, grew up around a stream known today as Cheonggyecheon.[2] Flowing roughly west to east, the stream cut across about seven miles in the center of the city. Over the centuries, the people of Seoul used the Cheonggyecheon the way residents of Detroit and numerous other cities have used their urban streams—as a sewer. During rainy seasons, nearby houses flooded and the sewer would backflow directly into the densely packed area. The city's death rate ran highest along the Cheonggyecheon.

The answer seemed obvious: enclose the stream in a large culvert and concrete over the channel to get rid of the smell, the flooding, and the other noxious effects. Planning began as early as the 1920s, but war and the high cost delayed major work until the 1950s. By the 1970s, workers had enclosed the stream and built an expressway atop the route. Then in 2002 a civic leader named Lee Myung-Bak ran for mayor on the issue of restoring the Cheonggyecheon. Critics lampooned the project as impossible. They said it would cost too much, displace shopkeepers doing business in the area, and lead to traffic jams once the expressway was removed. Voters thought differently. They elected Lee, accepting his vision of a greener city and a restored Cheonggyecheon as the key to making Seoul a twenty-first-century world capital.

Workers began tearing down the expressway and diverting the sewers in 2003. They recycled as much of the steel and other debris as they could. Yes, it was expensive; the actual physical construction ran into the many millions of dollars. But when completed a few years later, the Cheonggyecheon began to live up to the meaning of its name—Pristine Stream.

Today, the Cheonggyecheon is a center of civic pride in Seoul. New shops have opened along its edges. Travel agencies are booking tourist visits. Air quality has improved in the environs of the stream. The project won the prize for best public administration at the International Architecture Biennale in Venice, Italy.

And politicians everywhere please take note: Mayor Lee proved so popular for restoring the Cheonggyecheon that South Koreans elected him president of their nation in 2007.

THE QUAGGY

The Quaggy River flowing through southeast London, England, once served as part of nature's flood control system.[3] When rain swelled the flow, the river spilled over its banks into nearby fields. As people built up the community, they naturally didn't want to deal with flooding. So they buried the river, a move that forced the rushing water (and the flooding problem) farther downstream. Damage downstream could be extensive. A 1968 flood inundated the town center of the community of Lewisham. More recently, water three feet deep flooded fifty properties. Scientists told the community to expect such flooding on a regular basis, certainly every ten years and maybe more often.

In 1998, the community approved a plan to restore a portion of the Quaggy to a more natural state. Floodwater would find its way into natural catch basins upstream instead of flooding downstream in Lewisham. The plan envisioned restoring a 4.3-kilometer (about 2.5-mile) stretch of the river in Sutcliffe Park, where the Quaggy was buried under soccer fields.

Everyone in the surrounding area got involved. Unburying a river is not as simple as digging up the culvert and cracking open the concrete. Scientists surveyed the river's plants, trees, fish, birds, small critters, even the local bat population. Planners worked with local homeowners to design walls, garden features, and plantings along the newly restored river. Workers planted native flora, and nature restored a lot more on its own. Soon the banks of the Quaggy sported wildflower meadows, wetland terrain, reed beds, lakes and ponds, all home to a wide variety of wildlife. As a result, visits to Sutcliffe Park are up 73 percent, and people who visit the park say they now stay an average of three and a half hours longer each month. These visitors say they go to the park because it's a healthy thing to do.[4]

And if planners wanted above all to reduce flooding in the communities downstream, the Quaggy restoration worked a lot sooner than anyone expected. Just two months after the official opening of Sutcliffe Park in July 2007, the newly restored flood basin absorbed an estimated sixty thousand cubic meters of water. Homes and businesses downstream in Lewisham and nearby districts remained dry.[5]

ARCADIA CREEK

In Kalamazoo, Michigan, about three hours west of Detroit, a stream known as Arcadia Creek originally flowed from near the campus of Western Michigan University across the northern end of downtown to the Kalamazoo River.[6] Like the Cheonggyecheon and the Quaggy, it was prone to flooding during heavy rains. An earlier generation of Kalamazoo residents, like the people in Detroit and Seoul and many other cities, had turned their stream into a sewer. A later generation enclosed the Arcadia in a narrow concrete channel and buried it.

As downtown Kalamazoo built up, more and more ground got paved over, and with the creek buried, there was nowhere for rainwater to go—no natural drainage system to absorb a sudden rush of water. Water stayed on the paved surface and found its way into nearby basements. By burying Arcadia Creek and paving over the nearby land, Kalamazoo had created a hundred-year floodplain that covered most of northern downtown.

In a floodplain, property owners and developers find it difficult to get financing for new projects, and insurance companies are reluctant to write policies. So buildings on the north side of downtown Kalamazoo were deteriorating. Increased crime and the economic flight to suburbia after World War II worsened the problem. Historic architecture was being lost to abandonment and water damage. So with the rallying cry "Free the Creek!" Kalamazoo began planning in the 1980s to restore Arcadia Creek and correct the damage done generations earlier.

Dave Feehan, later the director of the International Downtown Association in

Washington DC, then served as president of the nonprofit Downtown Kalamazoo Inc. DKI helped pull together a coalition of local interests—a bank, a community college, two hospitals, and a few businesses—to come up with a way to pay for restoring the creek. Upjohn pharmaceutical company committed to building a research facility along the banks of a restored stream if the city used the increased tax money raised to fix the problems. That allowed Kalamazoo to form what's known as a "tax increment financing district" to capture and use the future tax revenues to pay off bonds issued to pay for the current project.

Some citizens complained about the cost of uncovering the creek, but engineering studies showed that a restored stream would handle flood-control duties for not much more money than it would take to improve and rebury the creek's culvert. Besides, initial public investment of eighteen million dollars leveraged more than two hundred million dollars in private investment. With the revenue identified, the city's newly formed Downtown Development Authority issued bonds, and the project got under way. Workers uncovered five blocks of Arcadia Creek, deepening and widening its channel. They built a series of weirs to manage the creek so that it still flows during dry spells but can expand during heavy rains. Workers created a pond and small park at the eastern end of the restored area to serve as a new downtown festival site.

Arcadia Commons, as the project is known, went on to win numerous awards. The project cured the flooding problem downtown, and a new museum was among several attractions to open along the restored creek. Activities at the new festival site generate an estimated twelve million dollars a year in sales and payroll for local businesses. And a creek that was buried for a half-century or more flows once again under the open sky.

When Dave Feehan considered whether the cost of the project was worth it, he said, "Absolutely. It took a lot of public and private money, but it paid for itself over and over. It's all in all proven to be a great stimulus for development, [and] it cured the floodplain. . . . Once in a while," he said, "you get things right."

Daylighting Streams

Phalen Wetland Park, the Cheonggyecheon, the River Quaggy, and Arcadia Creek may seem like isolated or extraordinary examples of cities going back to nature, but they're not. When a researcher named Richard Pinkham with the

Buried for a century or more, the daylighted Arcadia Creek runs above ground again in downtown Kalamazoo, Michigan. (Author photo)

Rocky Mountain Institute surveyed the field in the late 1990s, he found eighteen similar projects already done in the United States and two dozen or so more in various planning stages.[7] And those were only the ones he had time to look into. Europeans took the plunge with even more enthusiasm than Americans. Since 1988, the city of Zurich, Switzerland, has opened up twenty thousand meters, or about 12.5 miles, of previously buried streams in more than forty different projects.[8]

The technical term for uncovering a stream, pond, or wetland that has been buried is "daylighting." Enthusiasm for the practice rose in the United States after the daylighting of Strawberry Creek in a park in Berkeley, California, in 1984. That project drew much attention and led to similar ones. Daylighting is only one way to restore natural water features; people have polluted waterways, diverted their flow, hemmed them in with concrete culverts, and otherwise mangled their natural state without actually burying them, and repairing the damage often doesn't require uncovering a stream. However, daylighting's possibilities are among the most dramatic—but not dramatic in the sense that digging out a waterway produces another Mississippi River. A daylighted stream is more likely to flow as a trickle at times and to swell during rains, as do streams that have never been buried. Nor can we ever recover the pre-European-settlement ecosystem; too much has been done to the soil and streambeds, and even a daylighted stream will still have to compete with buildings and roads and other human artifacts.

What is dramatic, as we've seen, are the peripheral effects of daylighting. The process solves community problems by creating or restoring floodplains, and it boosts property values by creating a valuable neighborhood amenity. Daylighting can also create a new water hazard on a golf course or provide a new green corridor for strollers and bicyclists. Schoolchildren will find it a natural outdoor laboratory. Air and water quality can improve as the natural environment breathes freely again. Neighbors can build community relations rallying around a project that undoes the environmental harm done by a previous generation. In other words, daylighting can change a community in profound ways.

But the process is far from simple. As Joan Nassauer told me, daylighting requires a lot of expertise—soil specialists, plant specialists, hydrologists, civil engineers, urban planners—and, of course, the cooperation of neighborhood folks living and working nearby. And the complexity of these projects is only one barrier to getting them done. Nearby neighbors as well as city leaders might object to daylighting. Some will say uncovering a stream will create a nuisance—a breeding ground for pests, a place where small children might drown. Many will object to the cost despite the benefits. Since people may see nothing but a parking lot or an open field today, getting them to see the possibilities of daylighting a buried stream may require a long period of education.

We would commit an error, though, if we looked at daylighting merely as a technical, scientific, or even an economic challenge. No matter how difficult the tasks, the big question is always a political one—or, to raise the stakes even higher, a cultural one. Daylighting forces us to ask: Living in a place where our ancestors wounded the landscape, do we suffer today from those earlier actions? Can we lose a connection to nature and remain healthy humans? In cities such as Portland and Seattle in the Pacific Northwest, restoring streams crucial to the survival of the salmon speaks to the very identity of the community. To lose the salmon would inflict a psychic injury from which those places might never recover. Every city that's tried daylighting streams agrees: By mending our broken landscapes, we make an act of faith in ourselves.

WHAT CADILLAC FOUND

Restoring the Detroit ecology is a worthy goal, but first you need an idea of what to restore. What did the French find when they built their fort on the northern bank of the strait that we call the Detroit River in the summer of 1701? Let Cadillac himself tell it: "On both sides of this strait lie fine, open plains where the deer roam in graceful herds, where bears, by no means fierce and exceedingly good to eat, are to be found, as are also the savory wild ducks and other varieties of game. The islands are covered with trees; chestnuts, walnuts, apples and plums abound; and, in season, the wild vines are heavy with grapes, of which the forest rangers say they have made a wine that, considering its newness, was not at all bad."[9]

This pleasant land was cut by several streams to which the French and later settlers gave names: Savoyard, Parent's, May's, Knagg's and Conner creeks. These rose from various places in the area; one, the Savoyard (supposedly named for a native of the Savoy region) arose in a willow swamp on what is today Detroit's near-east side and flowed westward across what is now downtown, creating a popular fishing hole at Woodward Avenue. As was the trend of the day, early Detroiters threw their garbage and wastes into the streams. So foul did the streams grow that by the first decades of the 1800's Detroiters were covering them up to turn them into sewers.

Unseen for more than a century, Detroit's hidden creeks have nonetheless left their legacy. Wet basements are a notorious problem in Detroit. In the downtown area, would-be developers visiting empty buildings with hopes of remaking them into something new often find the basements filled with water. When David DiChiera, the legendary leader of the Michigan Opera Theater, first visited the old Capitol Theatre in the 1980s with hopes of remaking it as the Detroit Opera House of his dreams, he found a piano floating in the orchestra pit.[10] Drainage issues are compounded by that water just below the surface of

Detroit, pooled atop the dense layer of glacial clay. One can dig a hole almost anywhere in the city and hit dampness, if not actual water, within a couple of feet.

So, given that Detroit buried its streams long ago, given that burying them doesn't stop basements today from getting wet, and knowing what we know about Phalen Wetland Park and Cheonggyecheon and the Quaggy and Arcadia Creek, the question arises: With so much water so ready at hand in Detroit, why not make the most of it?

BLOODY RUN CREEK

A couple of small water-related projects have already taken place in Detroit. In the late 1980s and early '90s, the city of Detroit created Chene Park, a large riverfront music amphitheatre, and a small pond became part of the landscaping. Not far away, the state of Michigan in 2009 constructed a new wetland pond near the riverfront as part of its William G. Milliken State Park & Harbor. The wetland pond features native plants and grasses and educational displays on the usefulness of natural systems for dealing with excessive rainfall. Neither of these projects, though, can be characterized as daylighting, since neither restored natural features to the landscape. A lot of riverfront land consists of fill, put there by the city and by industrialists generations ago to firm up the waterfront for business purposes.

When it comes to actual daylighting in Detroit, only one project has drawn even moderate attention. That's the suggestion, often repeated but never acted upon, to daylight Bloody Run Creek. Among the rolling terrain in historic Elmwood Cemetery on the city's east side, one can catch a glimpse of Detroit's early topology: a small bit of what the French called Parent's Creek meandering along toward the Detroit River before disappearing below ground again. Ever since Chief Pontiac's warriors thrashed the British on the site in 1763, turning the stream's water red, Detroiters have known the small waterway as Bloody Run. Soon after the battle, Detroiters began using the stream as a sewer. Hoping to avoid cholera and other diseases linked to open sewers, the city began the process of burying Bloody Run Creek in 1875, working from the Detroit River north to the city's boundary at 8 Mile Road, completing the process decades later. Because of the gravesites established in the 1840s, Elmwood Cemetery

was never bulldozed flat in the twentieth century. Only that little stretch of
Bloody Run remains open today.

The idea of daylighting Bloody Run has seen many incarnations, but none
has been implemented as of this writing. As early as the late 1970s, a Detroit
architectural firm, Schervish Vogel Merz, began toying with the idea of restoring
a stretch of Bloody Run as part of a plan for linked riverfront parks. The idea
didn't pan out, but the firm reprised it in 1993, when it suggested a new park
with a daylighted Bloody Run as the centerpiece. The huge scope of the project
proved too daunting. Eventually, Steve Vogel, one of the firm's partners, became
dean of architecture at what is now the University of Detroit Mercy, and in 1995
he directed the school's Detroit Collaborative Design Center in a presentation
called "Unearthing Detroit." The presentation, as part of the exhibition
Empowering the City: New Directions in Urban Architecture, proposed the
daylighting of Bloody Run. Finally, the city-sponsored Community Reinvestment
Strategy in 1999 took up the idea of daylighting Bloody Run Creek as part of a
lower-east-side reinvestment strategy, but again the idea went nowhere.

Then in 2000, Vogel led an architecture studio whose plans went beyond
merely daylighting the stream to conceive of an entire urban village surrounding
a resurrected Bloody Run. Vogel and his team called the project Adamah, a
Hebrew word meaning "of the earth." Students taking part in the studio worked
with residents of the east-side district, careful to avoid the We're-the-Experts-
and-We'll-Tell-You-What-You-Need approach of so many previous attempts
to rescue Detroit. They worked particularly closely with Detroit's legendary
community activist Grace Lee Boggs and her Boggs Center to gather ideas.

What emerged was utopian by anybody's standard—a vision for a three-
thousand-acre community, about three times the size of Detroit's Belle Isle
Park, itself one of the largest urban parks in America. Daylighting Bloody Run
was the centerpiece of the Adamah project and would produce the expected
benefits of flood control and a more natural landscape, but the project went
beyond that. It envisioned an entirely self-sustaining community with a town
hall–style democracy and a walk-to-work economy based in part on wind farms.
The community would enjoy the latest voice and data transmission links,
and it would fill its energy needs by refining ethanol and using hydrogen fuel
cells. People would get around using a low-tech, Earth-friendly approach with

bicycles, shared community-owned cars, and a revived trolley system. Co-housing and other shared living arrangements would be available. The economy would include cooperatives and the trading and bartering of food grown locally for services. The Adamah community would get around Detroit's dismally failing public school system by creating home schools and new charter schools for the neighborhood.[11]

Utopian visions aside, the Adamah project is on to something when it envisions opening up Bloody Run. An old friend of mine, the late Karl Greimel, longtime dean of architecture at Lawrence Technological University, used to visit Elmwood Cemetery now and then, reveling in how it retained, as in a time capsule, something of Detroit's natural landscape. In the past, when a rapidly growing city buried Bloody Run and concreted over almost every available inch of land, restoring the original landscape wasn't feasible. But now, with so much of Detroit empty and going back to nature, it is feasible.

And it's feasible not just along an abandoned corridor like Bloody Run. If Seoul could daylight its Pristine Stream and Kalamazoo could open up its Arcadia Creek, each running through the heart of the city, why can't Detroit daylight its Savoyard Creek that runs beneath downtown? (I can hear the howls already from traffic engineers and city department heads.) Downtown Detroit remains woefully underused, even after thirty years of heroic stabs at revitalization, and the rising number of apartment and condo dwellers living downtown need neighborhood amenities more than anything else. If densely packed Seoul, with its population of ten million people, can rip out an expressway to restore a natural waterway, why can't shrinking Detroit uncover a few of its own pristine streams? If the city really wants to do something good downtown, it should stop building office buildings and find a way to daylight the Savoyard.

Daylighting is not easy, cheap, or a panacea for urban ills. But it's one more tool in the toolbox—a most interesting tool, and one that's aptly suited to Detroit's growing expanses of vacant land.

If nothing else, there might be a lot fewer wet basements.

6

FILLING THE VACANCY

Daylighting streams and reforming our roads offer just two approaches to revitalizing a distressed city. But we'll need to use multiple strategies to find productive and environmentally clean uses for Detroit's vacant urban landscape. In this chapter, we look at several more approaches to vacancy, from rescuing vacant lots to filling the space with forestry, artwork, and wildlife habitat.

RESCUING VACANT LOTS

The most basic unit of urban recovery is the vacant lot. So many of the tens of thousands of vacant parcels in cities we find interspersed—one here, two or three there—among still-occupied homes and businesses. Single vacant lots represent the starting point for recovery—or the harbinger of further decline.

In Detroit, the smaller house lots run around thirty by one hundred feet, hardly a great deal of land. That's not even one-tenth of an acre. But leave that single vacant lot to fester, and it infects the entire neighborhood—first the homes to either side or across the street, since no one wants to live next to or look out onto a weed-choked, debris-filled lot. In time, vacant lots can affect an entire street and even a neighborhood. Drive down any street in Detroit and look closely at the vacant lots, and you'll get a pretty good idea which direction that block is headed. Nothing remains stable; our neighborhoods get better or they get worse. To halt decline and to get neighborhoods moving in the right direction, we need to figure out some constructive uses for our vacant lots. Fortunately, a lot of smart people have been thinking about this very problem.

For many years, a neighborhood known as Northern Liberties in Philadelphia was the only zip code in the city to lack a public park. Picture a Philly street scene out of the *Rocky* movies—gritty brownstone homes lining one side of the street and mills and workshops lining the other. For decades, the 900 block of

North Third Street was home to the American Street Tannery, the sort of smelly business that can define a district. In the late 1980s, after the tannery closed, the U.S. Environmental Protection Agency declared the parcel a Superfund site and helped remove the structures. For a while it looked like new residential units might rise there. But those plans died, and the developer donated the site to the Northern Liberties Neighbors Association in 1995. Local residents found themselves the owners of what was now a two-acre vacant lot.

It was time, they decided, to create the park they'd always wanted. They envisioned not a passive park with lawns and a few benches, but a park with a purpose, or, rather, lots of purposes. Residents mapped plans for community gardens, a farmers market, and a performance platform to stage events. To get them started, a local nonprofit group gave the neighbors a $59,000 planning grant. The EPA chipped in $15,000 worth of soil testing to make sure vegetables grown there would be safe to eat. The Pennsylvania Horticultural Society helped with technical advice.[1]

A dozen years after they began work, residents today boast that their Liberty Lands park is the heart of a revitalizing community. Park amenities include a fully subscribed community garden with thirty-seven plots, sculpture by neighborhood artists, and a children's playground. At the lower end of the sloping site, a stage hosts musical performances. During summer months, the neighborhood association screens movies as part of its free weekly Lawn Chair Drive-In series.

Perhaps most interesting, the slope of the land was graded to create a small rain garden behind the stage at the lower end of the park. Like many older urban neighborhoods, Northern Liberties never enjoyed sewers adequate to deal with heavy rains. The combined stormwater and sewerage that couldn't flow through the city's system spilled instead into nearby rivers. By channeling the rainwater through landscaping, the water flows down into a cistern behind the stage from which trees, plants and grass drink their fill. "This is an old part of the city," Bob Grossmann of the nonprofit Philadelphia Green told me the day we visited the park. "The sewers here have always been challenged by the amount of stormwater. So this takes some of the pressure off the sewers." It's quite a package—locally grown vegetables, entertainment, a strengthened community bond, park views to enhance real estate values, even a boon for the environment.

When Northern Liberties neighbors created their park, they did themselves a world of good. They also demonstrated several of the most important ways we have to rescue vacant lots in cities. The most obvious way to stabilize a vacant lot—to prevent it from dragging down the values of adjacent homes and the wider neighborhood—is to cut the grass, collect the trash, and otherwise make it look cared for. Good neighbors in cities across the United States do just that, fighting blight with a lawnmower and hedge trimmer and maybe a paintbrush and a garbage bag.

Operating a notch above that volunteer level, the Pennsylvania Horticultural Society, the oldest such "greening" organization in the nation, has stabilized thousands of vacant lots in the city through the work of its Philadelphia Green program. When taking on an eyesore lot, the group collects the trash, gets rid of the weeds, and then imports a layer of new topsoil, the old dirt being usually too filled with demolition debris to support anything but weeds. The society plants new grass, perhaps a few trees, and erects a simple post-and-rail fence. These fences have become the trademark for the society's lot stabilization campaign, and it's bracing to see how much better a neatly mowed lawn and a simple fence looks than a weed-and-trash-filled lot. On the day that I drove around Philadelphia with Bob Grossmann to observe these tactics, he told me that the city government used to erect chain-link fences around some lots. That turned out to be a bad idea. The fences themselves looked ugly. The lots grew tall with weeds that nobody cut, and trash collected along the base of the fence. The society's simple wood fences, on the other hand, look inviting. The lots look cared for. It looks *intentional*.

A professor at the University of Pennsylvania named Susan Wachter studied how much good these greening activities did for local property values. Her report found that vacant-land improvements boosted surrounding home values by as much as 30 percent, which she called "an astonishingly large impact." New tree plantings alone raised housing values by about 10 percent. In Philadelphia's New Kensington area, that translated into a four-million-dollar gain in property value through tree plantings and a twelve-million-dollar gain through lot improvements.[2] Similar studies could be done in Detroit and other cities to measure the impact, but anecdotal evidence supports the belief that

Above: A vacant lot in Philadelphia before treatment by Philadelphia Green. *Below:* The same lot after treatment. (Courtesy Philadelphia Green)

Above: And another Philadelphia lot before . . . *Below:* . . . and after. (Courtesy Philadelphia Green)

fixing up vacant lots pays off almost immediately as neighbors begin to make additional investment in their own properties.

Nor does lot improvement cost that much. Bob Grossmann told me that Philadelphia Green can stabilize a vacant lot—topsoil, grass, trees, fence—for an initial cost of about $1.20 per square foot. They then maintain it by contracting with a landscaping firm to visit the lot fourteen times during the summer to mow the grass and pick up trash, all for twelve cents per square foot. To translate that into Detroit real estate, for a typical home lot in Detroit, one of those old 30-by-120-foot lots, we could stabilize it for about $4,500 and maintain it all summer for another $450.

The Greening of Detroit, the nonprofit organization that has been planting trees and rescuing vacant lots in Detroit since the 1970s, plants about three thousand trees each year in the city, using money from contributors and the sweat equity of volunteers. In Detroit's North End district, the area east of Woodward and north of Grand Boulevard, the Greening of Detroit has focused on eighty vacant lots out of the nine hundred or so in the neighborhood. Each week, they clean them up, plant shrubbery and trees, put in signage or bird feeders, and in general do something positive to help the neighbors see that somebody cares.

Paul Bairly heads the Greening of Detroit's tree-planting effort. "Often these lots don't look horrible; they've just been abandoned," he told me during a tour of the North End. "But they're often used for purposes that are fairly derogatory for the neighborhood: prostitution, drug sales." After volunteers led by the Greening of Detroit clean up the lots, the parcels become community meeting places, pocket parks. "It really gives them a chance to get out and see their neighbors," Bairly told me, "and it gives them a much stronger sense of community just by having those lots cleaned up."[3]

Robin Boyle, Wayne State University professor of urban planning, told me that many potential solutions to Detroit's vacant lots meet surprising resistance from traditional planners. The unconventional ideas lie so outside the normal range of planners' training and experience (trained as they are to manage growth, not decline) as to sound goofy on first hearing. Early in his tenure at Wayne State, in 1992, Boyle suggested to a group of planners that they consider something tried successfully in London, England—creating an artificial ski hill.

proposed Path
vacant lots
key spots
churches
schools
parks

Connecting the dots: students at a planning charrette in 2009 show how to link vacant lots together to form a greenway in Detroit's Villages district. (Courtesy the Villages of Detroit)

"'They built a ski slope,'" Boyle recalls telling the local planners. "'They've got this dirt. So they mounded it up, and they put that sort of carpeting on it, and they gave some kids some old skis and they go up and down this mud heap in the east end of London. Why don't we do that here?' And they looked at me as if I was crazy. I said, 'One thing you've got is a large amount of space and a large amount of dirt and a large amount of trash. Build a mountain. You have no topography.' And I remember the reaction, 'You're crazy!'"[4]

If we wanted a primer on all the different ways to rescue vacant lots, we couldn't do better than the Pattern Book put together as part of Cleveland's "Re-imagining Cleveland" effort. This booklet, an all-purpose strategy for turning Cleveland's widespread vacancy into a sustainable environment for the twenty-first century, includes an illustrated guide to dozens of ways to rescue vacant lots.[5] Among the techniques included in the pattern book is phytoremediation, which, as we saw in the chapter on urban agriculture, simply means using plants to extract contaminants from soil. Plants draw their nutrients from the soil; by planting them on contaminated sites, we simply ask the plants to suck out the bad stuff, too. That bad stuff can include lead, arsenic, and other heavy metals, petroleum-based substances, or pesticides—all the things you might find after a century or two of uses like the tannery that once operated in the Northern Liberties neighborhood. Experts say that spinach, Indian mustard, sunflowers, and cabbage are good accumulators, that is, plants that extract heavy metals from the soil and retain them within the plant tissues.

Phytoremediation gets a lot of attention these days. Often its advocates talk as if it represents one of Harry Potter's wands: just plant sunflowers and—poof!—your vacant lot has been cleansed like magic. Nothing's that easy, of course, and the dirtier the soil to begin with, the harder the cleaning job, and the bigger the bill. Getting rid of the plants once they suck up the contaminants can raise the cost, since they may have to be carted to a hazardous waste facility. Given all the variables, cost estimates have to be made one site at a time.

Both the level of effectiveness and the cost of phytoremediation depend on what type of toxicity is present and at what depth. For some vacant lots phytoremediation may represent all we need. Old industrial sites and defunct military bases have seen the most phytoremediation work so far, but neighborhood activists are using it more and more in vacant urban lots. Despite the quibbles about its effectiveness, many urban farmers and neighborhood activists hope and believe that cities can use phytoremediation as a tool in far more locations than they have to date.[6] And even if it takes a while to work, phytoremediation delivers side benefits along the way. Every time I pass a field of sunflowers, I feel a smile come to my lips, and I can't imagine I'm the only one.

Another way vacant lots can improve the lives of city dwellers is if we use them as sites for geothermal wells. They may seem like a brand new invention, but the Romans used geothermal wells to heat houses two thousand years ago, and animals have always dug burrows into the earth to find a more stable temperature than on the surface. Using geothermal energy involves tapping into the earth's inner heat, available just below the surface, and using it to our advantage. We can harness this heat energy by sinking a "well" (really a set of looped pipes that circulates a liquid solution) into the earth to a depth where the temperature remains a fairly constant 45 to 58 Fahrenheit. A geothermal system works using heat-transfer technology. In winter, the system pulls heat up from the earth to heat a house or other building. In summer, the system draws heat out of buildings and sends it into the earth.

Kent State's Cleveland Urban Design Collaborative Pattern Book suggests sinking geothermal wells in a vacant lot between two occupied homes to heat and cool the houses. The upfront cost tends to be high—about $42,000 per lot, so in a shared situation, each homeowner would pay $21,000—but the savings in energy costs can pay that back within a reasonable number of years.[7] Nor is it just adjacent houses on either side of a vacant lot that can benefit. In Klamath Falls, Oregon, geothermally heated water piped under roads and sidewalks keeps them from icing over in winter. In New Mexico and other states, rows of pipes carrying heated water help keep agricultural fields warm enough that frost doesn't kill the crops. Another positive byproduct to using vacant lots as sites for geothermal wells might be extending the growing season a month or two for Detroit's community gardeners.

Vacant lots can also serve as community parking lots. The American humorist Will Rogers once quipped that America was the only nation to drive to the poor house in an automobile. That can be a cruel joke when applied to low-income families who can barely afford bus fare. But the fact remains that cars are abundant throughout Detroit, perhaps because residents can't rely upon the city's troubled bus system, and rapid transit remains just a gleam in the eye of civic leaders. Parking all those cars requires space. And if nothing else, a vacant lot can offer another dozen or spaces off the street for the community to share.

The cost of a parking lot need not be prohibitive. Paving materials run about $1,500 per space, meaning that a twelve-space lot would cost $18,000 to pave. Add the cost of landscaping to soften the appearance of the lot, and you might come to a total of $25,000. Who pays for it? Some combination of neighbors and grants from community-minded foundations or other benefactors. If there's money left, and theft and vandalism are threats, a community can enclose the lot in a security fence with secured admittance.

We could go on. Solutions to vacant lots suggest themselves all the time, even if many of them sound, as Robin Boyle found, ridiculous on first hearing.

How about a putt-putt miniature golf course or a stage for neighborhood performers? Perhaps we could mound up some dirt to create a motorbike track, as residents did on vacant land in Detroit's Corktown district in 2009. The simplest of these solutions cost little and can be implemented by volunteers. The bottom line is that our vacant lots need not look as barren as they do. They can prove as fertile as our imaginations.

ART TO THE RESCUE

If any city has suffered as much abandonment as Detroit, that city is St. Louis. From a population peak of around 850,000 residents in 1950, the city now is home to about 350,000. The city has its share of boarded-up houses and empty office buildings. But St. Louis recently undertook one of the most innovative efforts to rescue a largely abandoned public space of any American city. That effort is known as Citygarden, a 2.9-acre sculpture park in the downtown's central corridor that opened in mid-2009. The cost of the park grounds ran to over $25 million, paid for by the local Gateway Foundation, and to that was added the work of twenty-four artists. The park includes a meandering 1,100-foot wall topped with Lake Superior granite that serves both as a defining edge and as a bench from which to view sculpture. A work called *Zenit* by Italian sculptor Mimmo Paladino presents a bronze horselike creature with a multifaceted starburst on its back. Polish sculptor Igor Mitoraj created a twelve-foot bronze head resting on its side. St. Louis's executive director of development, Barbara Geisman, said Citygarden will enhance the attractiveness of nearby development opportunities in the downtown area. "This is probably one of the best things that's happened downtown in the last couple of decades," she told the media.[8]

Other cities have attempted the same sort of thing, blending a more conventional park space with dramatic artwork to create a hybrid space, probably none better than Chicago's Millennium Park, built by decking over some open-air rail yards and featuring "the bean" (more formally known as *Cloud Gate*), a hugely popular sculpture by Anish Kapoor. Citygarden and Millennium Park demonstrate that cities with available land can use quality public art as one tactic in building a better city.

The Greening of Detroit park in Detroit. (Author photo)

Marilyn Wheaton, the former head of cultural affairs for the city of Detroit and now director of the Marshall M. Fredericks Sculpture Museum in Saginaw, says that public art can enhance the lives of residents in any city, distressed or not. "In an urban environment, public art tends to energize people as they pass it by," she told me. "Public art might honor a historic or contemporary person or event that is significant to the community. It might invite children in to play or learn or be creative."[9] Public art, she added, might be functional and provide shelter from the sun or the rain, like Andrew Zago's modernist piece in the Greening of Detroit Park on Jefferson Avenue. And a permanent work of civic art, Marshall Fredericks's *The Spirit of Detroit* at the city's Coleman A. Young Municipal Center, has served as the city's icon for fifty years. People gather for protests and prayer vigils beneath its outstretched arms, and the city playfully drapes the statue in a Red Wings or Pistons jersey when the local teams play for national championships.

Guerrilla art, created by often-anonymous artists on vacant lots or at abandoned factories, often pops up in cities like Detroit, where local artists vie to paint murals on sides of abandoned buildings. The quality varies from amateurish to semi-professional, but it has long ago been accepted as legitimate public art. The Detroit Riverfront Conservancy in 2009 engaged local graffiti artists to paint the bridge abutments that remained after an abandoned rail line was transformed into the Dequindre Cut greenway. This sort of artwork is often temporary, because it wears away as time goes by or gets demolished for new neighborhood projects, but it can enliven the street scene for as long as it lasts. One example turned up not long ago on Belle Isle, Detroit's large island park, when an unnamed artist used stones along the riverbanks to create small Zen-like rock formations. For a few happy weeks people enjoyed the works, and then a few disgruntled characters knocked them over.

The most famous guerrilla art installation is Tyree Guyton's Heidelberg Project in Detroit. Begun in 1986, the giant outdoor art installation marked Guyton's attempt to fight back against the abandonment that scarred his boyhood street, Heidelberg Street. Guyton and his volunteers, many of who were neighborhood children, gathered refuse from the streets and yards, painted it, and then piled it in vacant lots and around poles. They adorned houses and trees with ever-evolving splashes of color and texture.[10] Dennis Alan Nawrocki, the author of the book *Art in Detroit Public Places*, notes that the Heidelberg Project is even more remarkable given its grassroots origin versus the corporate or foundation money that supports projects like Millennium Park and Citygarden.[11] No one was ever neutral about the Heidelberg Project. It won numerous awards, yet the city of Detroit demolished parts of the art installation in 1991 and again in 1999. But the project continues to evolve and today remains a must-see tourist stop for many visitors to Detroit.

Artwork can thus fill up some of the vacant spaces in our shrinking cities. More important, it can fill up some of the vacant spaces in our souls. The most important projects, like Citygarden and Millennium Park, cost tens of millions of dollars and occupy prime downtown real estate. Smaller art installations, while they cost less, show a grittier face to the world, and often don't survive more than a season. But they represent something. Big or small, polished or not, public art demonstrates that, even in the most distressed cities, many still hope and work for better days.

The famous Heidelberg Project by artist Tyree Guyton in Detroit did more than fill up a mostly vacant block with colorful artwork. It inspired other artists all over town. (Courtesy David Clements)

TENDING THE URBAN FOREST

The term "urban forest" may evoke a picture of a vast wilderness, home to Daniel Boone or Robin Hood. Planners, though, use it to refer to tree cover of a more modest sort, the kind that exists within cities. Detroit, like many other cities, lost many thousands of trees to bulldozers during the great urban build-up of a century ago, and it also lost substantial tree cover years ago to Dutch elm disease and other ailments. Efforts to replace that tree cover remain under way in many cities; in Detroit, the nonprofit Greening of Detroit has planted about sixty thousand trees in the past quarter century or so, or about three thousand a year (one of those trees in Detroit's West Village district, I'm proud to say, was planted with the help of my own sweat equity). I'd like to argue that a civic policy of enhancing the tree cover—of restoring the urban forest to a much greater degree than we have done to date—offers a winning strategy for cities that find themselves getting smaller.

It's a no-brainer. Every schoolchild ought to know by now (even if many of their parents forget) that trees soak up carbon and thus mitigate global warming; that trees shade our homes and streets, cooling the urban heat island (cities typically run several degrees warmer than nearby rural areas because of car exhaust and heat rising from all that sun-soaked concrete and all those buildings); and that trees, being nice to look at and home to a variety of songbirds and other wildlife, help ease the tensions of big-city life.

Yet in all the hundreds of urban development presentations I have sat through as a reporter, trees have remained at best an afterthought. I'm sure that many thousands more trees have been destroyed during those projects than were planted as part of the fringe of greenery that developers like to tout. Now, though, with industry leaving and the urban landscape opening up for the first time in a hundred years, Detroit and other cities with a lot of vacant land enjoy an opportunity to restore the lost tree cover to a much greater degree than they've done so far. Detroit, of course, already sees miles of its vacant land returning to nature, and so the city may reap some of the benefits of increased tree cover without any effort. But that's hardly ideal. Such benefits can be characterized as accidental, which means they are more likely to go unnoticed and likely to be lost again at the whim of a developer.

Why are trees undervalued in development discussions? I think it's because all the benefits that trees give us, such as shade and songbirds, are things we count as free public goods. In general, our culture treats free things as unimportant, expendable. When trees are seen as expendable, it leaves them prey to developers and city leaders hoping to win votes with a big new project. By putting a cultural value on shade and fresh air and birdsong, we might understand the cost we bear by destroying our tree cover—a cost we'll go on paying later, long after the trees are gone.

The cost I'm talking about is not only psychic; it's literal, and it will hit us in our pocketbooks. In other words, if shade and cooling and carbon sequestration were not enough in themselves, we need to see that trees are also valuable. Real estate agents have long known that trees enhance the value of property, and some recent studies have attempted to quantify that. A study in the mid-1990s found that 85 percent of real estate agents believed a house with trees would be 20 percent more saleable than the same home without trees. One study looked at how shopping districts performed with or without large, well-maintained trees, and found that shoppers are willing to pay more for parking and stay longer in tree-lined shopping districts. It also found that customers believe the merchandise sold there to be of higher quality and worth on average 12 percent more.[12]

Those particular benefits accrue to individual shopowners and homeowners, but trees produce a financial gain citywide, too. To understand this, picture the parking lot of a suburban mall—all those acres and acres of asphalt. Not only does the lot radiate heat on sunny summer days, when rain hits, there is nothing to stop it from running down nearby storm sewers, first picking up whatever pollutants may be clinging to the surface of the lot. From the sewer, the water runs into a treatment plant, or, depending on the capacity of a system and how it's engineered, it may overflow into a nearby stream or river. Trees help reduce that stormwater runoff in a couple of ways. The leaves, branches, and trunks catch a lot of the rain and prevent it from getting to the ground, and some of that captured water evaporates back into the air. And, second, the soil in which the trees grow soaks up more rainwater. So trees reduce the volume of water running into a stormwater containment plant. That translates into fewer dollars spent by a municipality.

The total reduction in runoff depends on the density of the tree cover, but one study from Dayton, Ohio, found a 7 percent reduction in runoff with the existing tree cover there and suggested that a 12 percent reduction would be possible with just a slight increase in the number of trees. Studies by the nonprofit advocacy group American Forests suggest that impervious surfaces, like mall parking lots, increased by 20 percent in urban areas between roughly 1980 and 2000, costing taxpayers more than a hundred billion dollars in stormwater treatment costs. Meanwhile, a study in the Washington DC metro area found that the region's tree cover reduced the need for stormwater retention by 949 million cubic feet, valued at $4.7 billion over the twenty-year life cycle of a treatment facility.

Numerous cities worldwide already recognize how an urban tree cover saves municipal dollars. Stuttgart, Germany, once suffered from industrial pollution and traffic fumes to an unpleasant degree. The city implemented some pollution control measures, but also turned to a more natural form of air conditioning.

Cool, clean air flowed nightly down into the city from hillsides above, and the city learned that restricting development along the ravines that served as channels for the cool air, thereby preserving the trees on those slopes, kept those refreshing breezes flowing through. The Stuttgart approach got noticed elsewhere in Europe and was much imitated.

Studies and examples like these help us begin to put a dollar value on what the specialists call "ecosystem services." It's a relatively new field, and its newness allows more hardened development advocates to portray it as the tree-hugger lobby. We've got to change that. We know we value scenic views and that good views substantially increase the value of real estate. Curiously, though, that hasn't stopped us from bulldozing meadows and orchards, damming rivers, and burying streams. We take delight in songbirds and marvel that nature puts on such a show for us; yet the importance of wildlife, let alone the benefits of biodiversity and carbon storage in trees, is undervalued in urban development councils. If we expect to do better—to help Detroit and other cities take advantage of the opportunity that getting smaller affords them—we must begin to assert a dollar value for tree cover and other natural systems in any discussion of redevelopment goals.

Robin Boyle, the chair of urban planning at Wayne State University, urges cities to look to the urban forestry movements in Europe, which have demonstrated real financial benefits. "The model of urban forestry that evolved in Britain and in Europe has been pretty effective," he told me. "They've realized what the ground conditions need to be; they've realized what the types of trees need to be; they've realized the management of them; they've realized the way in which products can be harvested; they've realize the amenity value of urban forestry. So it's not a bad short-term model." Of course, the phrase "short-term" in the context of a forest means at least forty years. But Detroit's vast empty spaces enjoy the luxury of time. "Models that come from the urban forestry movements are ones that we should be paying a bit more attention to," Boyle said.[13]

How do we do that? The American Planning Association suggests that cities create municipal tree commissions that have a legal right to intervene in development planning (much as, say, design review committees now judge the architectural merit of a proposed development). Such a commission could help write and enforce ordinances that promote urban forestry, and it could sponsor awards to mark successes. This commission might be a quasi-governmental body, or the work might be contracted to a nonprofit entity like the Greening of Detroit or Philadelphia Green. Regardless, the body would have to have the clout to enforce its policies.

How to pay for a renewed forest cover in a city that can't afford to supply basic services for its citizens? There are examples from around the nation that suggest some ways. Olympia, Washington, uses a capital improvement fund derived from real estate excise taxes and utility taxes to pay for its forestry program. Salem, Oregon, pays for tree care with its portion of the state's motor fuel tax. Urbana, Illinois, uses fines to help pay for its program, among them the fines for motorists who damage trees in accidents. Urbana also sells composted yard waste back to homeowners to support its tree program, a bit of entrepreneurialism that brings market forces into play.

What's Good for Wildlife Can Be Good for Us

Just as we enjoy a scenic view, we enjoy seeing wildlife in its native habitat—at least when that habitat isn't too close to our own. Too close, and encounters with wild creatures can make any of us a bit nervous. I remember the first time I saw an opossum lingering near my van in the parking lot of our condominium building along Detroit's riverfront. Like many people, my initial reaction was to freak out a little. Opossums resemble big rats, with a sharp, pointy faces, thick bodies, and long tails. They tend to move slowly, so the critter didn't scurry away when it saw me; it mostly just stood staring at me. This was at night, and I kept my distance. Over the following year or so, I saw the opossum many more times, and I came to look forward to seeing it. How it sustained and sheltered itself amid the condos and co-ops along Detroit's Gold Coast, I never understood. When I no longer saw "my" opossum, I missed it.

Wildlife has been returning to Detroit in great variety. When workers at a DTE Energy power plant along Conner Creek on Detroit's east side noticed fallen trees and other signs of a beaver at work, one of their employees set up a trail camera that caught both still and video images of the beaver gnawing at a fallen tree trunk. The beaver's lodge was soon discovered nearby. John Hartig, an official with the U.S. Fish & Wildlife Service, confirmed that this was the first known beaver lodge in the city of Detroit in many decades; it was a tribute to efforts over many years to clean up the waters of the Detroit River and neighboring Lake St. Clair. When my newspaper, the *Detroit Free Press*, ran those photos of the beaver on the front page and the video on its website, www. freep.com, it created a sensation.[14] Even television host Regis Philbin mentioned the beaver on his morning show, and the audience gave a cheer.

The same trail camera also caught shots of a red fox and a pair of ring-necked pheasants. Pheasants long ago became common in the city, so common that the Michigan Department of Natural Resources around 1990 began trapping pheasants and releasing them in northern Michigan to mate with imported Szchuen black pheasants to create a hardier stock better suited to the harsh winters of the north country.

Eric Sharp, the outdoors writer for the *Free Press*, recently wrote of the morning he spent flushing pheasants with three generations of the Heck family—Jim, Jim Jr., and Jim III—who were training their hunting dogs along

11/29/08 12:02 PM

Captured by a motion-sensitive camera, a beaver goes for a meal in "urbanized" Detroit. (Courtesy Detroit Edison)

Above: The same trail camera caught a fox . . . *Below:* . . . and pheasants. Wildlife has found a new home in Detroit's empty spaces. (Courtesy Detroit Edison)

one of the abandoned corridors on Detroit's east side. On that beautiful October morning, Sharp wrote, they flushed fourteen pheasants in less than ninety minutes, and the Hecks apologized for what they considered a slow morning. "We normally bump up forty, fifty in a couple of hours," Jim Jr. told Sharp. "The numbers here are amazing. It's really wet this morning, so the birds are still holding under cover. They don't like to get wet if they can avoid it. And a friend took his dogs through here before we arrived."[15] The Hecks told Sharp the city's empty expanses returning to nature offered pheasants ideal cover for roosting, nesting, and feeding. The vacant areas sport tall brush and grasses that offer a smorgasbord for seed-eating birds and a lot of tangled places that provide good cover. Where there are pheasants, rabbits, and other small creatures, predators will follow, and Sharp and the Hecks saw four Cooper's hawks hunting that morning.

So far, the return of wildlife to the city, like the growth of grasses and trees on vacant lands, has happened by accident, a consequence of abandonment by humans. The question is, can reintroducing wildlife into cities be more than a byproduct of vacancy? Could it become a civic policy? And, if so, what would be the benefits?

Sometimes people living in cities consider wildlife a nuisance, and sometimes it *is* a nuisance. But wildlife restoration can offer a greatly enhanced biodiversity. We used to believe that humans and wildlife needed radically different living spaces. Now we understand that an environment appropriate for diverse wildlife—plentiful trees, clean water, open spaces—benefits us, too. A healthy natural environment not only makes us physically healthier, it helps us reconnect to nature. Ask anyone living in a pricy condo alongside a golf course. Those residents cherish their glimpses of deer and rabbits and nesting birds, and they delight in the melodies of songbirds. Could what's good for folks living alongside a golf course also benefit folks of more modest income in cities like Detroit?

When designing Phalen Wetland Park in St. Paul, Joan Nassauer and her colleagues aimed to create a place where smaller creatures—butterflies and songbirds and rabbits and the occasional fox—could find new homes. And, Nassauer says, you can scale a project to keep wildlife at that level. But we really achieve a greater biodiversity in the bigger patches where the native landscape has been restored. Deer actually like highly fragmented landscape, with lots of shrub-type plants. Some of the bigger birds—hawks and bald eagles—will return to the bigger swatches of restored landscape but not the smaller patches, such as a simple daylighted stream. "The big patches are more likely to host wildlife that people recognize as special," Nassauer says, such as birds of prey and beavers.[16]

Then, too, there's an economic benefit to restoring the landscape to serve as wildlife corridors: Taxpayers don't expect them to be maintained as they do a public park. Once mapped out and planted, you pretty much leave nature to nature. And as Nassauer points out, there exists a very simple planning device for keeping people out: just don't design paths through the denser, woodsy areas. The bordering edge of trees and shrubbery sends a message to stay out. In the more open, turfy parts of the wildlife corridor where residents can see across a good distance, that's where we put our walking paths to invite people to experience nature as something more than a view you see from a distance.

As we saw at Phalen Wetland Park, creating a denser natural environment doesn't prevent building new development right up to the edge of it. Indeed, the most popular new residential projects in many suburbs across the United States are precisely the ones that leave as much of the natural landscape intact as possible. A city can benefit economically by returning more land to nature even as it builds up other parcels nearby. A city can shrink and grow at the same time.

In this and previous chapters, we've looked at ways to revitalize the vacant and abandoned spaces within a city like Detroit. Approaches such as daylighting streams, road diets, and urban agriculture have already contributed to better-looking, more sustainable urban landscapes in communities coast to coast and in other lands. But finding new, healthy uses for these spaces will not, by itself, remedy all of a city's problems. A city without jobs is a city that will lack the resources to undertake these and other self-help measures. We also need to heal the wounded economy. We turn to that need next.

Revving the Urban Economic Engine

Along the Delaware River in Philadelphia, the Workshop of the World district used to manufacture scores of products. Back in the mid-twentieth century, most industrialized cities had similar districts. Then, jobs were plentiful and the economy churned out miracles of growth decade after decade. Now that the urban workshop era has passed into history, and jobs have been dispersed around the globe, cities like Philadelphia and Youngstown and Detroit struggle to find new engines for their economies. Luckily, there are ways to advance that struggle, techniques that work to jump-start the economies of shrinking cities.

An Ernest Hemingway character who was down on his luck explained that he had gone broke in two ways—slowly, and then quickly. That's Detroit's story. Detroit's economy had been faltering for a long time before the Great Recession of 2008–9 all but wrecked what was left of it. Years before, in 1984, the downtown Hudson's department store closed, and auto factories had been shuttering over many, many years. But the collapse of the nation's economy in 2008 plunged General Motors and Chrysler into bankruptcy and sent the city of Detroit's unemployment rate—the official rate calculated by the government— soaring to an all-time high of around 30 percent in mid-2009.[1] Even that appalling statistic didn't come close to capturing the depth of the crisis. As of autumn 2009, many Detroiters had stopped looking for jobs. Some never started looking or didn't know how to begin to look. The unofficial jobless rate at that time was probably at least 50 percent.

Then add to that the effects of the foreclosure crisis, which has cost perhaps fifty thousand households their homes in Detroit in the past few years.[2] That number approaches 20 percent of Detroit residences. The estimates vary as to how many people left the city as a result of losing their homes, but it is safe to guess that many did. Houses in some Detroit neighborhoods would sell for a dollar if a buyer could be found. The state of those residents left is dire: More than half the city's children live in poverty; half the adults cannot read adequately; and only 2 percent of Detroit Public Schools students were found to be college-ready by the 2009 ACT college readiness benchmarks.[3]

Against that backdrop, anyone reporting gleams of hope could be accused of terminal optimism. But in fact we do see glimmers of a new economy emerging in Detroit, albeit a tiny fledgling economy that could still wither and die like other hopeful signs have before. Yet should it succeed, this new economy will look very different from the economy of Detroit's Auto Century. It'll be small and nimble rather than big and lethargic. It'll answer more quickly to its customers than to Wall Street stockpickers. There'll be fewer suits and more khaki and jeans, and there'll be more local owners and fewer corporate downsizing experts.

A hundred years of depending upon all-powerful Ford and General Motors and Chrysler has left Detroiters ill-prepared for the rigors of a twenty-first-century marketplace. Detroit has plenty of smart engineers but damn few entrepreneurs. Yet this new economy will depend on entrepreneurs, just as the economies of Seattle and Silicon Valley have depended upon them for years. And by entrepreneurs I don't mean merely a few risk-taking owners. Our entire culture in Detroit needs to think more entrepreneurially, needs to value education and lifelong learning and the acquisition of new skills. We all need to think more about supporting local businesses, seeing the links between buying local products and services and prospering as a community.

Detroit's first task is to grow itself some locally rooted businesses. Detroiters know that corporate America has mostly abandoned them but for picking over the bones. The new firms will need to sustain a business model that doesn't depend upon making steel or cars and employing hundreds of thousands of blue-collar workers. And the new firms will have to band together to help each other in a way the business schools usually never teach and may not even recognize.

In the rest of this chapter we'll look at three types of business that could help create this new economy in Detroit and other distressed cities. The first type is the high-tech incubator. The second includes employee-owned and collaborative businesses. The third is social enterprise. Various other models can also boost a local economy, including the well-publicized tax incentives offered by groups such as the Detroit Economic Growth Corporation and the Michigan

Economic Development Corporation. But after a quarter-century of reporting on urban economies, I believe that these three less conventional ways of starting and nurturing businesses promise more results than do tax incentives. In terms of building locally rooted businesses that create jobs that stay in the community, these three models give a city like Detroit what it's lacked for so long: hope.

THE HIGH-TECH INCUBATOR

Five stories tall and designed like an early General Motors' concrete fortress, the building seemed a most unlikely place to begin Detroit's turnaround. In 2003, GM donated the long-empty structure to Wayne State University as the home of the school's newly established TechTown business incubator. I covered the ribbon-cutting for my newspaper in July of that year, and it seemed to me that GM had gotten the better of the deal. The structure looked like so many other abandoned auto plants I had seen in Detroit—a general air of clammy vacancy, open space defined by massive internal support columns, and concrete dust clinging to everyone's shoes. A previous attempt to establish a high-tech business incubator about a mile south of there some years before had fallen flat, and this TechTown thing, I suspected, was another example of hopes about to be dashed yet again.

Good thing I wasn't putting any money on that prediction. Today TechTown vibrates with entrepreneurial energy. It boasts five "graduates" already— successful start-ups that have moved on to their own larger facilities—and it is nurturing several dozen more start-ups at various stages of development. When I visited again in September 2009, crews were building a new wall in the lobby just to hold mailboxes for the growing number of member firms.[4]

No single person is responsible for TechTown's success, but Randal Charlton comes as close as any. An amiable, somewhat rumpled Englishman, Charlton started his career as a journalist back in London, writing about breakthroughs in agricultural technology for a London weekly. His beat involved reporting on how scientists in Europe and the United States were working to feed the world's hungry. He covered so many interesting advances that he and two friends started their own agribusiness consulting firm—the first of more than a dozen firms that Charlton would start over the years.

Once, he flew thirty-six pregnant jersey cows and "one rambunctious Jersey

bull" to northern Saudi Arabia, touching down on a desert landing strip and
successfully delivering the livestock to a sheik hoping to build up his dairy herd.
Charlton's contract called for him to merely deliver the cattle, but upon arrival
he and his partner saw that the sheik's existing herd suffered many ailments.
Many of the thousand or so cattle there were sick or dying. Cattle weren't
getting enough water, and their diet was out of balance. Many were suffering
as the result of standing in the sun during the heat of the day. So instead of just
delivering the cattle and flying back to England, Charlton and his partner stayed
for a few weeks to help the sheik as best they could. During the first part of their
stay, they weren't sure how much help the local people would accept from them.
Each night they dined late in the sheik's guest house, sitting cross-legged on
the floor and eating with their right hands from a common platter piled high
with rice and meat. Finally, after many dinners, they had established trust with
the sheik, and he asked Charlton if he could manage the entire herd for him.
In a few weeks, Charlton had sent dozens of skilled agricultural workers to the
desert, and soon these workers had doubled and then tripled the sheik's milk
production.

Charlton's most recent venture was Asterand, a biotech company that
supplies human tissue and human tissue–based research services to scientists
working to discover new drug therapies. Charlton told me that it was his search
for cheap, available research space for Asterand that brought him to Detroit,
where Asterand became TechTown's first client when the incubator opened in
2003. A few years later, Charlton left Asterand to take over TechTown itself as
its executive director. The incubator gets a lot of financial help from foundations
and Wayne State University and government agencies hoping to spark new life
in Detroit—ten million dollars' worth of such aid in 2009—and under Charlton's
direction TechTown is growing like sunflowers in summer.

Today, at seventy, Charlton exudes energy and enthusiasm for his fledging
entrepreneurs, who hatch their ideas at a remarkable pace. By autumn 2009,
TechTown counted 111 member firms in all. The number changes almost daily.
Not all the members were residents at the building known as TechOne; some
just use the address for their mail and come occasionally for the hand-holding
that TechTown's staff provides. But the variety among the member firms was

amazing. There were biotech firms like Asterand. There was an inventor who designed a device that will change traffic signals so that emergency vehicles don't have to slow down. There was an art restoration firm and a firm that imported art from South America. A consultant helped college-bound athletes work their way through NCAA rules regarding scholarships. There were logistics firms such as Cargo Solutions, which helps companies manage large delivery fleets; investment ventures such as iNetworks, a private equity firm specializing in funding medical devices and technology; and nonprofits such as Parent Child Computer Learning Foundation, which tutors Detroit school children.

Rent at TechTown is cheap, of course, and leases are flexible. Charlton himself has moved his office several times within TechTown since taking over as executive director when his space was needed more urgently by an entrepreneur. Some business incubators set a time limit for their tenants, telling them they have to move out after, say, two years, but TechTown takes the opposite approach. It encourages its entrepreneurs to stay as *long* as possible, until they simply outgrow the facilities.

"You've got to have a *culture* of entrepreneurship," Charlton told me. "Our challenge is not to disperse people with great entrepreneurial skills. It's to keep them close together because we've got to build this culture and knowledge of managed risk-taking. And that's key to it. I can't emphasize that enough."

Charlton likes to tell the story of John Stchur, a Certified Public Accountant who found himself out of work in 2002. Charlton was then working to start Asterand, and he interviewed Stchur and offered him a job. Stchur remained skeptical. He had no idea what a tissue biorepository was, and in any case he was not so sure he wanted another wild ride in a risky start-up. He had just lost his job with a high-tech phone company when the venture collapsed just before going public, a victim of the tech bubble bursting. As an experienced CPA, he could have easily moved back into the corporate world, having worked at Ford Motor Company and Price Waterhouse. But the lure of another start-up proved too strong. Today Charlton credits Stchur with fueling Asterand's growth, taking the company public in 2008, and winning kudos as the Chief Financial Officer of the Year in *Crain's* annual business awards. Charlton quotes Stchur as admitting, "I have always been a few months away from being out of a job. But

I suppose I thrive on risk, and I come from a generation that expects to change jobs every few years. I expect to have fun in my work and would have died of boredom if I had gone back into a big company."

Getting like-minded people like this together is TechTown's goal. To foster a mingling and cross-fertilization of ideas, TechTown organizes many types of forums for its tenants—a China business club, an India business club, a faith-based-business club. Wayne State University moved its technology transfer and patents office into TechTown not long before I visited (out of their oak-paneled offices elsewhere on campus, as Charlton put it) to make it easier for entrepreneurs to learn about the latest research discoveries being made on campus. Wayne State professors conduct about $250 million a year of sponsored research, and getting the fruits of that research into the marketplace as paying businesses remains one of TechTown's key goals.

Perhaps because Charlton is a newcomer to Detroit, or perhaps because he's been an entrepreneur most of his life ("I've had at least as many businesses fail as succeed," he says), he harbors no illusions about the auto industry riding to Detroit's rescue as it has so many times before. "The cavalry ain't coming," he says. "The cavalry is actually going to be leaving town." He remains absolutely convinced—and absolutely convincing—that his brand of entrepreneurialism is going to save Detroit one business at a time. "We're trying to make this an entrepreneurial *church* where people come and get a dose of what it's all about," he told me. "It's nobody's fault that for the last fifty years it hasn't been necessary to be an entrepreneur or to think like an entrepreneur" in Detroit. "We've got to change that," he says, "and we've got to change that quickly."

EMPLOYEE-OWNED COOPERATIVES

Not long before his death in 1942, Detroit's great architect Albert Kahn arranged to turn his business over to his employees. Some seven decades later, the Kahn firm remains one of the nation's most successful and longest-running employee-owned enterprises. About seventy of the firm's 270 architects, engineers, and support staff owned stock in the firm in mid-2009, and the ownership was "flat," meaning the top managers held no more than 10 percent of the stock, with the rest broadly distributed among the ranks. Chuck Robinson, Kahn's president, told me that employee ownership produces numerous benefits for the company, including greater employee loyalty and longevity. "It really works," Robinson says. "You have an active interest and participation in the firm."[5]

Employee-owned enterprises turn up in places we may not suspect. Detroit's famed Lafayette Coney Island, a small downtown eatery favored by everybody from federal judges to homeless people, is employee owned and has been since its original family owners moved on.

The benefits of employee ownership can be substantial. Let's look to Ohio, which has lost about a third of its manufacturing jobs since 2000. There, employee-owned manufacturing companies helped by the Ohio Employee Ownership Center at Kent State University lost only 2.5 percent of their jobs over the same period. Across all sectors of Ohio's economy, employment dropped 5.5 percent since 2000, but the ninety or so firms in the OEOC network *increased* employment 9 percent. Profitability at the Ohio employee-owned firms beat the statewide averages, too, says John Logue, a Kent State professor who leads the center.[6]

It makes sense that employee owners work harder and track every dime more closely than employees at many other firms. The question now is whether fostering an atmosphere where workers find it easier to buy or start employee-owned firms can help cities like Detroit dig out of their seemingly bottomless economic hole. Deborah Groban Olson, a Detroit attorney who has spent her career helping employees buy and run their own companies, believes the answer is yes. She created the nonprofit Center for Community Based Enterprise in Detroit and for the past couple of years has been trying to match Detroit's great depth of engineering and manufacturing talent with entrepreneurial ideas that could turn into employee-owned businesses.[7]

A little background. Like the Albert Kahn experience and Lafayette Coney Island, if most firms are going to transition to employee ownership, they do so at the point of generational change, when the founder dies or retires. Often the children of a founder prefer to go to college and work in professions in which they're not required to work fifty-five or sixty hours a week like Dad did or go into the shop on Sunday afternoon to deal with every crisis. Many firms die at that point of transition; they liquidate or sell to competitors interested only in customer lists or in cherry-picking equipment. As more people go to college each generation, that loss of family-owned companies can get worse. The rate of transfer of businesses from the first generation to second generation, which used to be about 30 percent, has fallen to between 15 and 20 percent, and from second to third generation has fallen from 15 percent to 5 percent. John Logue, the Kent State professor who heads the Ohio Employee Ownership Center, says this point of transitional change coincides with a huge amount of pain. "We know that a failure to plan for ownership succession is the number-one *preventable* cause of job loss in the U.S.," he says.

If employees do get to take over the firm, good things usually happen. Profitability rises, Logue says, because "the workers don't eat their seed corn. They reinvest and grow more." Profitability also rises because the management ranks are thinner; in a workshop, you don't need as many supervisors because the workers are all interested owners. Corporate perks all but disappear, too, in employee-owned companies. Of the ninety or so firms in the Ohio network, Logue says, two sold their corporate jets and one sold its corporate helicopter upon becoming employee owned.

Such benefits have inspired attorney Deb Olson and other believers in the power of employee ownership to go from merely helping owners and employees work through a transition—as Albert Kahn himself did seventy years ago—to looking for opportunities to play matchmaker. Her goal is to put good business concepts together with out-of-work engineers and other talented people in Detroit. As of mid-2009, Olson said she had five good business ideas in need of talented people to work them; she and her Center for Community Based Enterprise would provide the legal expertise to help them get started. But she wasn't looking for out-of-town investors to come in, steal the ideas, and make a profit far away. She wanted to start the businesses right in Detroit. "It's the focus on working together and being rooted," Olson told me. "So we define community-based enterprise as any for-profit or nonprofit that has a sustainable revenue model, is committed to being rooted locally, and pays living wages."

What employee owners need, though, is a lot of help setting up a business and understanding the complex array of legal, financial, and managerial challenges that await them. That's what Olson in Detroit and Logue in Ohio and other enthusiasts hope to provide—a catalyst or information source to help workers take good ideas and convert them into business plans. "There's a lot of expertise that comes out of tool-and-die shops that used to belong to Ford and General Motors that could start new businesses, very easily in fact," Logue says. "My guess is in any major auto plant shutdown, you could probably start somewhere between five and ten new businesses that have a decent chance for success."

Community-based businesses that operate on their own can have an impact, but Olson raises another intriguing possibility: What if we multiplied the impact of each employee-owned firm by bundling a bunch of them together into cooperative arrangements? Co-ops use their shared production and buying power to command greater economic clout in the marketplace. The nation's agricultural sector is filled with co-ops. The Michigan Milk Producers Association, founded in 1916, is a member-owned-and-operated dairy cooperative with about 2,300 individual dairy-farmer members in Michigan, Ohio, Indiana, and Wisconsin. The National Council of Farmer Cooperatives, established in 1929, now represents some 2,500 farm co-ops across the United States with a total business volume in 2006 of $125.5 billion and total employment of over two hundred thousand people. Outside agriculture, though, co-ops are more rare in the United States, and we have to turn to Europe to see the full range and power of co-ops in action.

Italy is one center of cooperative economic arrangements. The concept was implemented after World War II. The co-ops originally grew from the gathering of produce, like grapes for wine. Numerous small farmers put their products together, made wine (or whatever) and shared the profits. It was much more efficient than having each farmer try to sell a few hundred bottles of his own wine. As time went by, the concept spread to having grocery stores in which local producers sold their items together at a lower cost of distribution.

Today in Italy's regions of Tuscany and Emilia-Romagna, co-op stores sell everything and anything: food, books, televisions, cell phones, bicycles, and on and on. The co-ops today run quasi-banks that function like credit unions. Members can take out loans, make investments, and have accounts where the interest rate is a bit better than it would be if they went to a commercial bank. They've also organized construction companies and other businesses based on the co-op model. Indeed, so widespread and successful are the co-ops that in some parts of northern Italy they're almost too successful—building mega-shopping centers on the outskirts of historic towns that compete with the small, locally owned shops, much as Wal-Mart is accused of doing in the United States. Despite that friction, co-ops are so numerous and powerful that Italians refer to them as a third sector of their economy, equally powerful with the public sector (government) and private sector (individual private businesses). Dr. Valentino Castellani, the mayor of Turin, Italy, from 1993 to 2001, told me that Italians view co-ops as a moderating influence on their economy, helping stabilize employment, among other benefits.[8]

For another dramatic example of successful cooperatives, look to Spain. The Mondragon Cooperative traces its history to the mid-1950s, when a priest named Don José María Arizmendiarrieta arranged to put local people to work in a small factory making oil stoves and paraffin heaters.[9] Today the Mondragon cooperative is a socially conscious business group consisting of more than 250 companies organized in three areas: finance, industry, and distribution services. The cooperative today employs some hundred thousand workers taking in some twenty-five billion dollars a year in revenue. Co-op activities range from retail stores to research in nano-technology. The co-op educates 7,200 students in its own schools and returns 50 percent of profits to its worker members.

The co-op idea as a tool to rejuvenate ailing cities is just starting to take hold in the United States. The Mondragon example inspired the creation of the Arizmendi Bakery in San Francisco in 1997, named for the enterprising Spanish priest. A cooperative bakery in Berkeley, California, called the Cheeseboard helped Arizmendi get started. The workers at the two shops have continued to share their knowledge, and two other Arizmendi bakeries have opened in the Bay area since then.

In Cleveland, three employee-owned cooperative businesses were getting started in 2009 as part of the Evergreen Cooperatives movement. One was the Evergreen Cooperative Laundry, a state-of-the-art, six-million-dollar plant catering to health care facilities, including nursing homes and hospitals. Another was Ohio Cooperative Solar, which was planning to install solar panels on the roofs of the city's largest health, education, and municipal buildings. A third company, Evergreen City Growers, was preparing to build and operate a hydroponic greenhouse with the capacity to produce three million heads of lettuce and almost one million pounds of basil each year.[10]

No ordinary laundry, solar company, or urban farm, the Evergreen co-ops stem from efforts by Cleveland's anchor institutions—businesses such as the Cleveland Foundation, ShoreBank Enterprises, and the big hospitals and universities in the city—to use their collective buying power to nurture the fragile economic life in the Cleveland Circle district. That district is Cleveland's poorest, indeed one of the poorest in the nation. The Cleveland Circle area is almost entirely African American; unemployment there runs very high; and there are relatively high numbers of felons returning to the community. These anchor institutions spend annually about three billion dollars a year on supplies and services of all kinds, yet not one penny of that was getting spent in their home district. So the Evergreen Co-ops are an attempt to channel some of that spending into city neighborhoods, not as charity but as payment for goods and services. The anchor institutions, along with John Logue's Ohio Employee Ownership Center at Kent State, and others, created the Evergreen co-op idea. For example, the anchor hospitals and universities will lease their roofs to Ohio Cooperative Solar and in turn buy the electricity produced by the rooftop panels. Within a few years, Ohio Cooperative Solar and its worker-owners hope to create the largest expanse of solar panels in the Midwest and be doing business far from Cleveland Circle.

Evergreen marks the first attempt to harness the economic clout of the city's anchor institutions to rebuild the city's economic base. Up to now, these institutions thought they had been discharging their civic duties simply by being there, building new buildings and paying their taxes. But operating amidst such stubborn poverty eventually led creative people to come up with a better idea. And so the cooperative model emerged.

Can such a model help Detroit? No doubt, but the process of setting up both employee-owned businesses and cooperative arrangements is complex. It requires a commitment not by a single hospital or university but by state and local governments, too. Tax policies need to tilt in favor of employee-owned and cooperative businesses, making, say, the transfer of a firm from a family owner to the workers simpler. One idea, for example, might allow a family-owned company to divert payments scheduled to go to the state's unemployment trust fund into an account to help employees buy their companies. State-backed loan guarantees for employees buying their firm upon an owner's retirement are another good idea. "This needs to be a part of public policy," John Logue says. "It's problematic if you put it off in the nonprofit fringe. There are a whole range of things you can do if you decide this is going to be part of the solution to our current misery. But it's going to take a policy choice on the part of state government."

Deb Olson agrees. "Detroit has been the seat of the biggest global corporations in the world for a long time, and we based our economy on that," she told me. "But they're in trouble, and to the extent that they're growing, they're growing elsewhere. So the focus of this is to say, we have to start looking at how do we, in a grassroots way, make a local economy here?"

Social Enterprise

Every now and then, I leave my desk at the *Detroit Free Press* and stroll over to Woodward Avenue to buy an ice cream at the Ben & Jerry's shop. I'm partial to Cherry Garcia. The shop measures a modest few hundred square feet, which rates as small compared to some of the ice cream emporiums in the suburbs. But customers find their way there, and all in all, this little Ben & Jerry's succeeds as well or better than most of the retail on Woodward.

Ben & Jerry's presents an example of social enterprise, a trend also known as social entrepreneurialism or more-than-profit business. This is where nonprofit work collides with for-profit motives, or, to use the catchy slogan of the field's advocates, it's where mission meets the marketplace. Social enterprises achieve social ends through business means, or, more simply, the promoters of social enterprises help homeless, abused, addicted, and otherwise troubled people by creating jobs for them when no one else will.

Goodwill Industries, the nonprofit group best known for running second-hand clothing stores around the country, owns and operates the Ben & Jerry's on Woodward. Ben & Jerry's Co. operates or licenses a lot of stores around the country, some of them operating like the one on Woodward as what the company calls PartnerShops—ventures where a nonprofit like Goodwill, rather than a for-profit investor, owns and operates the shop. Profits go back into the store or to support Goodwill's other ventures to help the poor, instead of to investors concerned only with the bottom line.

Social enterprises go far beyond ice cream shops. In the San Francisco area, a business-oriented philanthropic fund called REDF contributes money and expertise to more than a dozen social enterprises, including a T-shirt company called Asbury Images ("rebuilding lives one shirt at a time") and Pedal Revolution, a local bicycle store. The Wisconsin Women's Business Initiative Corporation has supported hundreds of local start-ups since the 1980s; it operates Coffee with a Conscience shops in Milwaukee offering only certified fair-trade, organic coffee. Besides its Ben & Jerry's on Woodward, Detroit's Goodwill runs a janitorial company that has a contract to clean the Detroit Zoo, and it runs a computer recycling firm that contracts with Dell. Goodwill also handles recycling for DTE Energy, the local power company. Lindsay Chalmers, the head of Goodwill's social enterprise ventures in Detroit, says the various enterprises employ five to six hundred people a year in the city. "In today's day and age, those of us who are going to try to produce a benefit for the community are literally having to produce the business models that will employ people because there *are no jobs* in our area," he told me.[11]

The Social Enterprise Alliance, a trade group representing social entrepreneurs, says the field today includes retail; service and manufacturing businesses; providers of social and human services; fee-based consulting and research services; housing construction and financing; and even technology enterprises. Like the Ben & Jerry's on Woodward, many if not most of these businesses operate as "normal" firms do, with many customers not even aware they're dealing with a social enterprise. "Sometimes, when people pass a person on the street who is down and out, they think, 'That person should get a job,'" writes Carla Javits, president of REDF in San Francisco. "But how many of us would offer them a job? The social enterprises that we support actually do."[12]

Running a social enterprise, even one as seemingly simple as an ice cream shop, can pose challenges that for-profit firms don't face. High turnover is a fact of life for social entrepreneurs; in fact, high turnover is the whole point, since enterprises like the Ben & Jerry's shop on Woodward want to move as many at-risk teens through the program as possible. But constant turnover means shops don't get the benefits that come with having veteran employees. Sometimes, though, social enterprises can turn disadvantages into a plus. A social entrepreneur named Jim Schorr found that out when he opened a Ben & Jerry's in the San Francisco area. His inexperienced teen workers were dispensing more generous scoops of ice cream into each cone than the business model allowed. That contributed to a cost of materials that was about 5 percent higher than in a typical Ben & Jerry's. Schorr used a peer-to-peer remedy to address the problem. He found that by getting the more experienced teens to train the newcomers, the operation saved money *and* created a good development exercise for the youths.[13]

Social enterprises usually benefit from subsidies not available to for-profit stores. Ben & Jerry's waives its franchise fees and all royalty fees for the PartnerShop stores, a benefit worth many thousands of dollars. The company also provides nonprofit operators with an annual travel stipend for training programs. And newly opened retail stores, in Detroit as in cities across the United States, often qualify for tax incentives and other help from city, county, or state governments, the amount depending on how badly civic leaders want the retailers to set up shop.

If the comparison of the Ben & Jerry's on Woodward with for-profit stores isn't exact, it doesn't need be to prove our point. We all know that Detroit can't count on the old auto plants and steel mills to do the hiring. And some of us are honest enough to admit that Detroit can't count on the next photovoltaic plant or advanced battery facility or Google or Yahoo to swoop in and shower new employment on the city, either. It may happen, but it's not likely. So Detroit, if it's going to see new jobs, has to create them on its own, and social enterprises offer a promising way to do that.

All three of these models—the high-tech incubator, employee ownership and cooperative arrangements, and social enterprise—overlap to some extent. Start-up companies can graduate from a high-tech incubator to join a cooperative, and social enterprises can become employee owned. I don't mean to draw sharp lines between the models, rather to suggest the range of hopeful efforts now under way in cities across America.

I know that a teen dipping ice cream for pocket money does not equate to generations of workers supporting their families on factory paychecks. Nor should we expect these new-model businesses to come trouble free. Like any businesses, owner-operators must deal with multiple problems, from a collapse of the national economy to teenage employees who scoop too much ice cream into a cone. Only the naive would believe that having your heart in the right place guarantees a profit. But having your heart in the right place does guarantee a level of energy and commitment that goes a long way in cities like Detroit and Cleveland. For those of us hoping to revive the urban economy, TechTown, Evergreen Cooperatives, and Ben & Jerry's don't seem like such bad places to start. Bill Gates learned computers as a gawky kid in his high school's computer lab. Who's to say that the next great entrepreneur can't get started scooping ice cream? Stranger tales have been told in the annals of American business.

8

THE BEST IDEA DETROIT'S NEVER TRIED

I first met Dan Kildee at a Starbucks coffee shop midway between Detroit and his hometown of Flint, Michigan. While writing stories for the *Detroit Free Press*, I had been hearing his name from more and more people who described him as the most important innovator in the urban redevelopment field. His job as the elected treasurer of Genesee County (the county with Flint at its center) seemed a fairly modest perch from which to garner so much praise. So I asked for an interview. Kildee, as people had told me, was a big, genial Irish-American pol. To break the ice I mentioned all the good ink he was getting about his work, and he laughed. "You pick an obscure enough topic, you can become an expert on it," he joked.[1]

Such self-deprecatory humor aside, Kildee in fact has become the face and the voice of one of the few truly new and important trends in urban redevelopment. If the single biggest intellectual leap we've made is accepting that getting smaller can prove an opportunity for cities, perhaps the single most important tool to make smaller cities work is the land bank. And that's Kildee's passion. At the beginning of 2010, Kildee resigned his elected post to become head of a Washington DC–based national nonprofit group called the Center for Community Progress, whose mission it is to help cities deal with issues of foreclosure, land banks, and vacancy.

We may as well distinguish up front between a land bank and the more general process known as land banking. First, all cities own property, and in healthy cities this property consists mainly of land for civic uses—parks, playgrounds, city halls, police and fire stations, jails, schools, and the like. In troubled cities (which include not only Detroit and Flint but what are by now other familiar names—Cleveland, Pittsburgh, Philadelphia, New Orleans, and on and on), city governments also own lots of land that once rested in private hands. Municipalities take ownership of these parcels through tax foreclosure. In truly distressed places like Detroit, the volume of land held by the city can prove enormous. The city of Detroit alone owns somewhere around forty thousand once-private parcels of land, mostly vacant lots, empty houses, and old factories. To hold on to this land in hopes of redeveloping it one day is known as land banking.

In the years after the Detroit riots of 1967, land banking got a dirty reputation. Conspiracy-minded citizens believed the city was allowing neighborhoods to rot for the benefit of wealthy suburban developers who one day would swoop in, grab all the land assembled for them by the city, and make a killing off it. The city of Detroit, of course, like other distressed cities, was doing nothing of the kind; it had simply proved too weak to stop its citizens from fleeing town. Detroit and other cities became land bankers not by preference but by default.

An entity like the Genesee County Land Bank, though, is a much different thing. A legal entity set up under state statutes, a land bank is a legal authority that can take ownership of a municipality's abandoned land and deal with it in some productive way. It can assemble land for redevelopment, or sell it off to people ready to put it back on the tax roles.

Now, if that's all a land bank did, it would be more or less indistinguishable from a city's previous land-banking role—taking possession of tax-foreclosed property and selling it off as need arose. It was Kildee's stroke of genius (and, as he modestly points out, the genius of a bunch of legal and urban-development experts working with him) that a land bank could do so much more—that a land bank could, in fact, prove a sort of urban alchemist, turning worthless, abandoned vacancy into redevelopment gold.

It worked like this: When Kildee took his post as county treasurer in 1997, he inherited the same system most other municipalities use, that of auctioning off supposedly worthless tax-foreclosed land each year to raise some revenue. That process left him dissatisfied. As someone who likes to tinker with systems, Kildee began to talk to folks about wringing the inherent value of real estate from these vacant parcels. After all, he thought, land is land—there's no more of it, and if you sell it to some speculator in a tax auction—some TV infomercial watcher in San Diego who's flipping properties from his laptop like he'd buy or sell penny stocks—that buyer can't pick up the land in Flint and move it to California. The problem, Kildee told me that day over coffee, is that urban leaders typically think of their tax-foreclosed land as used-up, disposable assets, something that no longer has any realizable value, that sadly has served its purpose and now just needs to be written off, taken off the books.

How to unlock the value that any real estate has within it? That's the question Kildee pondered. He talked to experts like Frank Alexander, a law professor at Emory University and a leading thinker on urban land issues, and Doug Kelbaugh, then dean of architecture and urban planning at the University of Michigan, and Bob Beckley, a professor in that school. And they tinkered and schmoozed and came up with an idea. What if, they asked, we took the "worthless" tax-foreclosed land in abandoned neighborhoods in Flint and put it into the same pot as more valuable tax-foreclosed properties in the suburbs? Suburban residents sometimes fell behind on their property taxes, too, but their properties generally were more valuable than parcels in the city. Genesee County was accumulating land in Flint—vacant lots and burned-out houses and empty factories—but it was also piling up some better parcels in the outlying suburban areas. Auctioning it all off to the highest speculator bidder each year just meant selling it to tax scavengers who often as not lost it themselves to tax foreclosure within a couple of years. Maybe there was a way to wring more value by treating the more valuable and less valuable land in a unified way.

As it happened, Michigan had recently changed its law on tax foreclosure, so that parcels seized for delinquent taxes now went into the possession of the county treasurer, not the local city. So Kildee as Genesee County Treasurer suddenly found himself in possession of a lot of parcels. He used the powers he and others found under existing Michigan law to create the legal authority known as the Genesee County Land Bank. Then he conveyed all the county-owned, tax-foreclosed properties to this new authority. And he himself became chairman of the Land Bank.

Having formed the Land Bank, Kildee began selling off some of its parcels—the more valuable ones in the suburbs—but not at auction, and not to speculators and tax scavengers. Instead, the Land Bank listed those properties with Realtors who sold them in the conventional way, one at a time, for a price more commensurate with their current market value. Pretty soon, the Land Bank had cash coming in. And Kildee took that cash and turned around and used it to spruce up the supposedly worthless parcels in Flint itself. The Land Bank demolished houses in Flint that were beyond repair or blighting an otherwise good neighborhood, and it paid for repairs to many others. Within the first five years, the Land Bank had demolished about a thousand eyesores in Flint and renovated about three hundred other properties, using the cash it raised from the sale of better properties in the suburbs. In effect, a little suburban value was being transferred to the inner city, even as the suburban parcels went back on the tax rolls and remained productive.

Kildee also sparked a downtown revival by using Land Bank cash to fix up a wreck of a building and moving the Land Bank's offices into the renovated space. Soon owners to the right and left were fixing up their buildings, too. The Land Bank provided incentives to developers to renovate the long-dormant Durant Hotel, located on a prominent overlook in downtown Flint. The eight-story, 250-room hotel was built in the 1920s; the Land Bank incentives have helped turn it into residential units.

Kildee's version wasn't the nation's first land bank authority. St. Louis had started the nation's first land bank as far back as 1971. Cleveland followed with its own version in 1976, Louisville, Kentucky, in 1989, and Atlanta, Georgia, in 1991. But it was Kildee's creation of the Genesee County Land bank in 2002 that opened the floodgates and introduced the very model of what a land bank should be. Since Kildee, with urban land expert Alexander as his theoretical guiding light, created the Flint area's land bank, some fifteen to twenty other municipalities have followed suit, among them Omaha, Nebraska, and Valdosta, Georgia. But Michigan's land bank law remains the strongest in the United States, Frank Alexander told me.[2]

To those who questioned the Land Bank's actions, Kildee could point to a Michigan State University study that bolstered his assertions of a land bank's value. The MSU researchers estimated that the Land Bank's actions had boosted property values throughout Genesee County by more than one hundred million dollars. And Kildee got more ammo against critics in 2007 when the Kennedy School of Government at Harvard University named his Land Bank the winner of its annual Fannie Mae Foundation Innovations Award for the best new idea in urban redevelopment.

When state lawmakers in Lansing, Michigan, decided to revise the tax-foreclosure law again, Kildee used the opportunity to do some more tinkering, helping state lawmakers rewrite the land bank authorization. As long as they had the hood up, Kildee said, they might as well fix a bunch of other things. The new law included a provision that any property owned by a land bank, which meant potentially any tax-foreclosed property, was by definition a brownfield (a polluted, abandoned tract of land), thus making all of a land bank's parcels eligible for brownfield tax credits. And, perhaps most important, the legal changes now allowed a land bank to seek a clear title to its parcels by authorizing a judge to do a mass action—in effect, to declare that a land title was "clean" with no prior holders having any further rights to it. That ability to scrub titles clean in a mass action proved a massive step. The often interminable process of clearing title to abandoned properties in a city like Flint had now been compressed to a mere few months.

Frank Alexander told me that a land bank needs to have quasi-governmental powers, although some newer land banks operate as nonprofits. The key power is the ability to waive or forgive delinquent taxes. He calls that power waving the magic wand to make land useful again.[3] Sometimes, Alexander said, a land bank may prove the wrong tool for a particular urban problem. Sometimes a city just needs better code enforcement or a better political climate so that leaders are willing to tackle their vacant land issues. And if a city creates a land bank just to hold land and not do anything with it or just to sell it off to speculators to make a quick buck, that city isn't accomplishing much.[4]

The Genesee County Land Bank is a model of its kind. In canceling the annual treasurer's tax auction of foreclosed properties, it created a healthier method of dealing with abandoned urban land. As John Kromer, an urban expert from Philadelphia, notes, auctions of tax-delinquent land bear little relationship to neighborhood plans or strategies. "Bidders at the public auction are not screened or pre-qualified with respect to their expertise as developers or their ability to improve and maintain the properties they acquire," Kromer says. "In many cities, the highest bid is about all that matters."[5] Kildee agrees. "The biggest single effect that we've had is we've cut off the supply of low-value land to speculators," he told me in one of our interviews. "It's hard to measure in some ways, but it's probably the single most significant effect that we've had."[6]

By selling only to more qualified and competent buyers, the Land Bank ensures better outcomes for all. Here's a startling statistic: Prior to the creation of the Genesee County Land Bank, around 80 percent of all properties sold through the county's tax-foreclosure auction slipped into foreclosure again within a few years. But as of 2009 as I was writing this book, the Genesee County Land Bank had sold off about 1,500 properties for more than six million dollars, and only a handful of those properties, fewer than a hundred, have come back to the county through a subsequent tax foreclosure. "It's an economic model as much as it's a land-use model," Kildee said.[7]

Kildee's Land Bank enables a city to accomplish the kind of projects everyone agrees it needs without the fuss usually attendant on redevelopment. Like many cities, Flint hopes to green some of its abandoned parcels, and the Land Bank allows it to do that. Kildee drove me around Flint to show off some of the Land Bank's successes, and we stopped at one lot where an eyesore had been removed and crews were establishing a rainwater garden and a pocket park. "It's a lot easier to make those decisions in the public sector as the *owner* of the land than to try to create inducements or regulations that produce the outcomes that you want to have produced," Kildee said. "In our case, we don't have to induce some private developer to do the right thing, we don't have to try to regulate private land use to create affordable housing integrated into market-rate housing. We just decide that's what we're going to do."[8]

Skeptics point out that Kildee enjoyed an unusual, if not unique, vantage point as both Genesee County Treasurer *and* chairman of the local land bank. In cities lacking such a strong and creative personality, or where the county treasurer balks at turning over tax-foreclosed properties to the land bank, the model might accomplish much less. Short-sighted political expediency can kill a land bank quicker than anything.

Kildee also cautions against inflated expectations. The land bank can provide a useful tool, but it's not a cure-all, any more than downtown aquariums and casinos and festival marketplaces proved magic elixirs in all those cities that followed those trends. The land bank can make good things happen, but the public-private partnerships it forges, like the one remaking the Durant Hotel in downtown Flint, still must meet the test of market reality. "I can't get somebody to put their own money at risk for something that the market would completely reject," Kildee told me.[9]

Such caution is worth taking into account in every attempt to create a land bank elsewhere. But with nearly ten years of operation under its belt, the Genesee County Land Bank has proven its worth and provides a model for hard-hit communities everywhere. It's ironic that Flint, a city so distressed it became a national symbol of urban agony in Michael Moore's film *Roger and Me*, is now viewed everywhere as a model of urban innovation.

As soon as Genesee County showed how useful a land bank might prove, a group of nonprofit activists in Detroit formed the Coalition for a Detroit Land Bank.[10] Those efforts got under way in 2005, but over the next couple of years the Detroit City Council refused to buy into the idea, despite exhaustive lobbying by the nonprofits. It came down to power. In Detroit, unlike many other cities, the city council doesn't have much real power, but one control it does exercise is over sales of city-owned land. The city owns tens of thousands of parcels of tax-foreclosed land, and the council must approved the sale of each and every parcel. Council members don't do this in bulk. To sit through the average Detroit City Council meeting is to be numbed by tedious detail. You wonder: Do these people really need to approve the sale of every vacant lot and derelict house? It makes no sense, until one remembers that controlling that huge inventory of land translates into power.

When the coalition proposed a land bank, some council members took it as a threat to one of their few powers, since establishing a land bank in effect meant ceding ownership and control of the land to the new authority. Council Member JoAnn Watson in particular opposed anything that appeared to limit Council's meager powers. It didn't matter that the council could set up all the guidelines for the land bank—that it could set the prices for the sale of lots and determine in advance which buyers would get first crack at parcels. No iteration of the coalition's proposal survived.

There it sat for another year or two. In 2008, council finally passed a watered-down version of a land bank as part of the city's application for federal Neighborhood Stabilization Program money, since the Feds were encouraging land banks by then. As of the end of 2009, this new land bank was still getting organized and had yet to hire permanent staff. But even when it gets going, it will operate only in the city and will not be able to leverage the value of properties in the suburbs, because city and Wayne County officials have failed to agree on anything remotely resembling a unified land bank. Therefore the Detroit model will not enjoy any of the features that distinguish Genesee County's successful model. As of this writing, it looks like Detroit's version will do little more than serve as a conduit for sales of the parcels the city already owns. One city department director told me that his plan once the land bank started was to sell off the city's foreclosed parcels as quickly as possible—the antithesis of the thoughtful process employed in Flint.

Robin Boyle, the professor of urban planning at Wayne State University, believes that the depressed values of Detroit real estate will further reduce any benefits gained by this neutered version of a land bank. For a land bank to work, there have to be buyers willing to pay for the land coming out of the land bank. Values are so low for Detroit's vacant and abandoned properties that buyers simply don't exist for much of it. "Absent a transaction, tell me how a land bank is going to do anything for the city of Detroit?" Boyle asked.[11]

So there it stands, as of late 2009. The idea of a meaningful Detroit land bank, an authority with real power that can emulate the success of Genesee County's model, seems stillborn. Meanwhile, cities across the nation are looking to Michigan for instruction on creating their own land banks—one of the best and most creative ideas to hit urban redevelopment in decades. But they're looking to Flint—beat-up, broken-down Flint—and not to Detroit. "Unfortunately," Kildee told me, "people in my business think about one year, because that's the budget, or two or four years, because that's their term of office. If we don't think about the next twenty or twenty-five years, we're going to make mistakes."

9

WHO GOVERNS?

As cities plan to creatively downsize—to move the few remaining residents out of blighted areas into more densely populated, economically healthy districts—a critical question emerges: Who decides? The answer that Youngstown, Ohio, supplied was simple. *Everyone* gets to be in on the planning, particularly the people most touched by changes. Moving out of a distressed district must remain a voluntary choice. Youngstown, as we saw earlier, may encourage, even nudge, a reshaping of the urban fabric by offering tax breaks and other incentives. But the city won't force anybody to live through a repeat of the urban renewal saga of the 1950s, when bulldozers leveled entire neighborhoods in the name of progress.

I take up this question of who governs because it must be addressed before we come to a close. Making the most of all that we've discussed will require a democratic process that includes everyone in the decision-making. Here's the rub, though: During this democratic process, a city still must provide the basic services expected of a municipal government. A city that cannot govern itself is a city that can only fail to make desperately needed changes. The city of Detroit has demonstrated that it can no longer even meet payroll without deep service cuts and significant layoffs. If city hall officials can no longer do all that we expect of a city government, who will?

The answer that's emerging in Detroit and elsewhere may be called a third way, beyond government and the private sector. Cities have long experimented with privatizing certain tasks—janitorial services, say, or garbage pickup—but in Detroit and other cities now we're evolving a new model of civic leadership, new ways of making decisions and providing services that once were thought the province of city hall. Detroit's extreme condition may have pushed it further along the road to this new model of governance than other troubled cities. In Detroit today, a range of quasi-public groups now do many things city governments used to do, from sweeping the streets to building and maintaining parks.

This new model, responsible for much of the progress in Detroit of recent years, blends corporate clout, cash from foundations, and a nonprofit management structure. City government still plays an important role, but civic leadership is shared between many different institutions. The Kresge Foundation donated tens of millions of dollars to build the Detroit RiverWalk, and the nonprofit Detroit Riverfront Conservancy oversees the RiverWalk and the Dequindre Cut. The Detroit 300 Conservancy built, maintains, and operates Campus Martius Park for the city. The Community Foundation for Southeast Michigan is the region's leading sponsor of greenways, putting up significant dollars for the Dequindre Cut and working with dozens of other potential sites. The Skillman Foundation works with neighborhood groups, and the C. S. Mott Foundation supports urban agriculture initiatives. The quasi-public Eastern Market Corporation operates Eastern Market, and other quasi-public corporations run the Detroit Institute of Arts, the Detroit Historical Museum, and other functions once run directly out of city hall.

Further, the nonprofit Greening of Detroit organization, rather than the city's virtually nonexistent forestry department, plants trees on Belle Isle and throughout the city. If Detroit actually gets a new light rail system downtown, as appears likely at this writing, credit will go at least as much to private citizen John Hertel and his quasi-public regional transportation planning committee as to anything that the Detroit Department of Transportation has done. And the Roger Penske–led Downtown Detroit Partnership, a private civic group, has taken over some street-cleaning duties as part of its Clean Downtown initiative.

Although fraught with political sensitivities, the privatization of traditional city functions is a trend that has gone too far to ignore—and one that Detroit should continue to encourage. Charlie Williams, a former top aide to Mayor Coleman A. Young and now president of an environmental firm in Detroit, told me that the inability of the city's bureaucracy to move quickly motivates the switch to a more private governance model. The fact that these new organizations exist implies, he said, "that the government doesn't do an effective job in terms of efficiency. The word the mayor used to always use was 'muscle-bound,'" he continued, "like a guy that's a weightlifter. He's so strong he can't throw a punch. You're overwhelmed by the bureaucracy."[1]

Take the RiverWalk as an example. In 2002, when work began, the Detroit Riverfront Conservancy was created to oversee the building and operation. Major backers included General Motors, the owner of the Renaissance Center, and the Troy-based Kresge Foundation. The city has been an important player, but just one of several in the effort. Desire to avoid Detroit City Council meetings and the circus atmosphere that sometimes prevails there may motivate some of these privatized solutions. Why undergo a public scourging by grandstanding council members when one can work quietly and effectively with a nonprofit conservancy or a foundation?

If the city's disappearing tax base, political bickering, and straitjacket regulations underpin the push for a more private governance model, disgust over political corruption gives it still more speed. The city is broken in so many ways, and the corruption of a Kwame Kilpatrick, the former mayor jailed for perjury, and a Monica Conyers, the former President Pro Tem of the city council who pled guilty in a bribery scheme, give urgency to the search for new models of civic leadership.

The trend toward a more private or quasi-public governance model has long sparked debate at city council meetings over whether the city was losing control of jewels like Eastern Market or, potentially, Belle Isle, which some would like to cede to the Huron-Clinton Metroparks system. But even as many people resist the trend, many leaders, in and out of city hall, admit there's little alternative to further evolving a new governance model given the bleak outlook for city finances. "There's always going to be some sensitivities with issues like this," Doug Rothwell, president of the nonprofit Business Leaders for Michigan (the former Detroit Renaissance) told me during a 2008 interview. "I think it gets back to making sure the public interest is met. These are public assets and public services, and you have to do those in a very responsible way."[2]

Even some of the most effective work that Detroit's city government undertakes is done through its own quasi-public arm, the Detroit Economic Growth Corporation, an outside agency that reports to the mayor but also has its own board and staff. During the RiverWalk project, DEGC President George Jackson negotiated the removal of cement silos that had long dominated the east riverfront, and the DEGC fixed up roads and infrastructure in the district. But the Kresge Foundation, General Motors, and the nonprofit Riverfront Conservancy also took leading roles.

Rip Rapson, president of the Kresge Foundation, told me in 2008 that a healthy city hall is still crucial, since some functions, like enforcing building and zoning codes or building roads and sewers, remain a municipal job. "You simply cannot substitute for public institutions that are well led and can marshal the sort of resources that move a community forward," he told me. "I think only the public sector is ultimately held accountable to the public, and that's both an advantage and a disadvantage."[3]

Yet everyone acknowledges that new ways of doing things have become essential. "Business can't be done the way it was ten, fifteen years ago," said Faye Alexander Nelson, president of the Riverfront Conservancy. "Communities are finding themselves in a much different situation now from the economic standpoint. Everyone has had to step back and really focus on the 'we': 'What are we going to do to create sustainable communities?'"[4]

With leadership getting more diffused all the time, many of these new centers of civic power reflect different opinions about what should be done and how. That leads to friction at times. Unlike political squabbling, this friction among the private and nonprofit leadership almost never breaks into the public media and general discussion. But it's there, and it's real. At the neighborhood level, many community development organizations (CDOs) in Detroit feel left out of the new decision-making matrix. They complain that foundations and other citywide nonprofits are picking winners and losers, favoring some districts and some CDOs over others. Nor is this complaint restricted to Detroit alone. In Cleveland, the Local Initiative Support Coalition (LISC), a nonprofit group that channels funds and expertise to neighborhood CDOs, pulled out of that city a few years ago over such conflicts.

Adding to their angst, many of Detroit's small community development corporations have lost their way in the Great Recession that began in late 2007. In the 1990s, many CDOs had earned some hard-won expertise building new housing in their districts. By scraping together whatever funds they could from foundations, government housing agencies, and private donors, many CDOs built rental apartments, senior centers, and even market-rate condominium projects. Indeed, until 2006 or so, many neighborhood groups had redefined themselves as housing developers. The housing crash that began in 2006 put an end to that, and it left many of these neighborhood CDOs with no clear mission, no money, and, in a practical sense, no one in city hall to tell their troubles to.

Listen closely and we can also detect some tremors of disagreement among the citywide nonprofits, foundations, and conservancies. Areas of interest and expertise can overlap, and personalities, as in any walk of life, sometimes clash. Take nonmotorized transportation plans. Multiple groups are trying to implement nonmotorized pedestrian and bicycle paths in the city. Just a partial listing would include the Kresge Foundation, which put up the big cash to build the city's RiverWalk; the Riverfront Conservancy, which handled construction of the RiverWalk and manages the waterside promenade; the Community Foundation for Southeast Michigan, which promotes the creation of greenways throughout the Metro area; and the nonprofit Michigan Trails & Greenways Alliance, which also tries to promote nonmotorized links in the city. Overlay a level of municipal and quasi-government regulation and pressure from the neighborhood groups who want to be at the table, and it's no surprise that unelected leaders squabble as much as elected ones.

But the debates among the many new private and quasi-public leadership groups shouldn't obscure what's happening in Detroit and, to some extent, in America's other distressed cities. It's not just the great expanses of empty land that define Detroit today, nor the abandoned factories, nor, for that matter, the vibrancy of Eastern Market on Saturday morning and the elegance of some fine old neighborhoods like Palmer Woods and Indian Village. The way Detroiters run their city is changing before our eyes, and the more we know about that, the more we encourage healthy methods and manage the change in new and creative ways, the better Detroit will be.

CONCLUSION

The Way Forward

An old joke holds that when in doubt, predict the trend will continue. Detroiters better hope that doesn't come to pass. The current trend in Detroit, in the depths of its calamity, portends only more abandonment, bankruptcy of city services, and economic distress. A city where one in three people is out of work and one in two is functionally illiterate has passed the tipping point and is heading inexorably to ruin.

Unless . . .

Unless we heed some of the lessons from Youngstown and Turin and Seoul and Cleveland and Kalamazoo and many other cities that arrested their decline or, at least, have put up a good fight. The people of these cities and many others have learned that healing the land, nurturing community-based companies, and revamping how we govern can pay off in stronger, healthier communities. The urban heroes we've met in this book—Iris Brown and Dan Kildee and Jay Williams among them—demonstrate that innovation is not only possible but also can be successful across a range of problems and locations. Even Detroit can boast more than a few success stories: The RiverWalk, Earthworks Urban Farm, and TechTown all would have seemed improbable not so long ago. Today they're part of Detroit's present and future.

So what kind of city *could* Detroit become? It could be greener, first and foremost, with more greenways and bicycle lanes and community gardens and a landscape much easier to navigate on foot and on two wheels rather than four. Ironically, higher population density would create a more walkable city. Densely packed urban neighborhoods attract retailers, so a city that builds up its healthier districts and connects them with greenways would be one where residents can find much more of what they need close at hand. Right now, shopping requires Detroiters to get in their cars and drive miles to find the stores they favor. Some day, as Detroit nurtures its local food economy and its local markets, they may be able to walk or bicycle and leave the car at home.

Increased density will be a key to Detroit's future redevelopment—not houses built on individual lots with big backyards, but neighborhoods packed with lofts and townhouses and high-rise units with enough people to attract the attention of retailers. Detroit's residential housing model, based on neighborhoods of small wooden single-family houses, will need to evolve for the city to prosper. If nothing else, the demographic trends are pushing us in that direction, as an aging population gives up the huge homes in the suburbs in favor of something smaller and more manageable. It's no accident that when the city cleared out the cement silos from the east riverfront, the residential projects slated to replace them were all multi-unit condominium dwellings.

Cocktail party conversation is likely to change, too. Back in the 1980s, every social gathering I attended resonated with the talk of automotive workers, mostly engineers, and the gossip about Ford and General Motors and Chrysler was inevitable. As the city's economy evolves into more community-based enterprises, those conversations will range over a broader spectrum of topics, including (if we're lucky) the life sciences and other entrepreneurial ventures. If lawmakers retain the state's lucrative movie incentives, which already has brought swarms of movie crews to the city, Detroiters may even be chatting up filmmakers at block parties and Sunday brunches.

The city will certainly lose more people, at least for a time. Detroit's 2009 population, depending on which estimate one accepts, hovers between 800,000 and 900,000, and will shrink some more. No one realistically can expect anything else. But if we see the opening up of Detroit's landscape as an opportunity and not a calamity—or, perhaps, as an opportunity wrapped within a calamity— we may achieve some good from it yet. As Valentino Castellani of Turin, Italy, says, "A crisis can be an extraordinary opportunity for change and innovation. Paradoxically, the deeper the crisis, the bigger the chance to change and innovate."[1]

I make no pretense that Detroit will ever see two million residents again or wield the economic clout it did during the Auto Century. But I believe Detroit can embody a gritty success, all the same. As the nation struggles to cope with rising global temperatures and soaring fuel prices, Detroit may emerge as the city that figured it out first—how to use its open lands to foster a local food economy, how to create a network of greenways that permits its residents to park their vehicles, how to help community-based entrepreneurs create a financial safety margin for a city once yoked to global economic swings. This future city may be home to no more than five hundred thousand residents, but it can function as a world-class city all the same, just as cities smaller than Detroit today enjoy worldwide fame, from Vancouver to Venice.

The years ahead will not be easy for Detroit. I would count it a miracle if they were anything but agonizingly difficult. But the way forward emerges from the efforts we see already under way—the greening of the city, the rise of a new entrepreneurial class, and the willingness of so many people to think and act in new ways. Keep it moving forward, and Detroiters may yet say, as Dorothy did when she woke up back in Kansas, *There's no place like home.*

GETTING INVOLVED

URBAN AGRICULTURE

Numerous groups offer opportunities to get involved in urban agriculture. For a national perspective, visit the American Community Gardening Association at **www.communitygardening.org.**

In Detroit, start with the Garden Resource Program Collaborative, a coalition of several farming groups including the Detroit Agriculture Network and Earthworks Urban Farm. Visit the website at **www.detroitagriculture.org.** Many groups, such as Earthworks, need volunteers at harvest time. All people are welcome. To learn more, visit Earthworks at **www.cskdetroit.org/EWG.**

To learn more about Kami Pathukuchi's SEED Wayne program, **visit www. clas.wayne.edu/seedwayne.**

Many other cities offer similar gardening programs. In Philadelphia, visit Philadelphia Green at **www.pennsylvaniahorticulturalsociety.org/ phlgreen/index.html.** For Milwaukee and Chicago, see Growing Power at **www.growingpower.org.**

GREEN TRANSPORTATION

Many groups are working to create nonmotorized transportation options in Detroit and other cities. To learn more about their efforts in Michigan or about volunteer opportunities, start with the Michigan Trails & Greenway Alliance, a clearinghouse for green efforts, at **www.michigantrails.org.**

To learn more about the city of Chicago's effort to promote bicycle transportation, visit **www.chicagobikes.org.**

RESTORING VACANT LOTS

Many of the groups that work on community gardening also work on vacant lot restoration. For Detroit, start with the nonprofit Greening of Detroit at **www. greeningofdetroit.com.** For Philadelphia, visit Philadelphia Green at **www. pennsylvaniahorticulturalsociety.org/phlgreen/index.html.**

URBAN FORESTS

Reforestation programs offer one of the best ways for citizens to help their communities. Groups like the Greening of Detroit and Philadelphia Green need hundreds of volunteers each year to plant and maintain trees. All it takes is some sweat equity and a few hours on a Saturday morning. To learn more about these programs, visit the Greening of Detroit and Philadelphia Green online (see above).

Chapter 1

1. Jeff Kunerth and Linda Shrieves, "Central Florida Is Shrinking; Orlando, Orange County and the State Saw Populations Dip for the First Time in Decades," *Orlando Sentinel*, August 20, 2009.

2. Karina Pallagst, "Shrinking Cities: Planning Challenges from an International Perspective," in *Cities Growing Smaller*, vol. 1 of *Urban Infill*, ed. Steve Rugare and Terry Schwarz (Kent, OH: Cleveland Urban Design Collaborative, 2008), 5–16.

3. The details in the following two paragraphs come from Thorsten Wiechmann, "Strategic Flexibility beyond Growth and Shrinkage: Lessons from Dresden, Germany," in *Cities Growing Smaller*, vol. 1 of *Urban Infill*, ed. Rugare and Schwarz, 17–30.

4. Kildee interview with author in Auburn Hills, Michigan, on February 20, 2009. Kildee is the former treasurer of Genesee County, Michigan (1997–2009). In 2002, he founded the Genesee County Land Bank and acted as its chairman and CEO from 2002–9.

5. United States Census data.

6. Joan Nassauer, interview with the author, March 4, 2009.

7. John Gallagher, "Fortunes Can Look Up After Auto Losses, Detroit Told," *Detroit Free Press*, September 19, 2009.

8. The entire Youngstown 2010 plan can be found online at www.cityofyoungstownoh.com/about_youngstown/youngstown_2010.

9. The information and quotes from Jay Williams in this section come from an interview with the author on September 18, 2009.

Chapter 2

1. Robin Boyle, interview with the author, Wayne State University, December 15, 2009.

2. Thomas Morton, "Something, Something, Something, Detroit: Lazy Journalists Love Pictures of Abandoned Stuff," *Vice* August 2009: 1, www.viceland.com/int/v16n8/htdocs/something-something-something-detroit-994.php.

3. Florent Tillon, interview with the author, Detroit, June 9, 2009.

4. John Gallagher, "Detroit: Land of Opportunity: Acres of Barren Blocks Offer Chance to Reinvent City," *Detroit Free Press,* Dec. 15, 2008.

5. Tobias Armborst, Daniel D'Oca, and Georgeen Theodore, "Improve Your Lot!" in *Cities Growing Smaller*, vol. 1 of *Urban Infill*, ed. Steve Rugare and Terry Schwarz (Kent, OH: Cleveland Urban Design Collaborative, 2008), 45–64.

6. Ibid, 48.

7. Alan Mallach, interview with the author, Detroit, April 22, 2009.

8. John Gallagher, "Urban Villages in Detroit's Future?" *Detroit Free Press*, May 22, 2009.

9. Mallach interview, April 22, 2009.

10. Christine MacDonald, "Council to Sue Over Cobo Plans," *Detroit News*, March 10, 2009.

11. Nolan Finley, comments made on *FlashPoint*, WDIV-TV, Detroit, March 8, 2009.

12. Jennifer Dixon, "Backlog Plagues Home Program: Hundreds of Detroit Homes Need Rehabilitation But Millions in Funding Goes Unspent," *Detroit Free Press*, March 23, 1998.

13. Editorial, "End Barriers to Detroit Demolition," *Detroit News,* February 1, 2002.

14. David Ashenfelter and Joe Swickard, "Kilpatrick Ties Cloud Reform," *Detroit Free Press,* July 25, 2009.

15. Margaret Dewar, "Selling Tax-Reverted Land: Lessons from Cleveland and Detroit," *Journal of the American Planning Association* 72, no. 2 (2006): 167–80.

16. Sue Mosey, interview with the author, Detroit, June 12, 2009.

Chapter 3

1. The story of *Las Parcelas* is based on the author's site visit July 8, 2009. See also H. Patricia Hynes, *A Patch of Eden: America's Inner-City Gardeners* (White River Junction, VT: Chelsea Green, 1996), 71–79.

2. The historical survey of urban gardening is based on Laura Lawson, "The Planner in the Garden: A Historical View into the Relationship between Planning and Community Gardens," *Journal of Planning History* 3, no. 2 (2004): 151–76.

3. Ibid, 155.

4. Jerry Kaufman and Martin Bailkey, *Farming Inside Cities: Entrepreneurial Urban Agriculture in the United States*, Lincoln Institute of Land Policy, 2000.

5. A good survey of the Havana experience can be found in Bill McKibben, *Deep Economy: The Wealth of Communities and the Durable Future* (New York: Times Books, 2007), 71–77.

6. Will Allen's story is summarized on the John D. and Catherine T. MacArthur Foundation website at www.macfound.org/site/c. lkLXJ8MQKrH/b.4537249. See also Growing Power at www.growingpower.org.

7. Will Allen, "About Us," *Growing Power, Inc.*, www.growingpower.org/about_us.htm.

8. The description of Earthworks Urban Farm is based on author interviews and a site visit on September 12, 2009. See also www.cskdetroit.org/EWG.

9. Ashley Atkinson, "Fostering Citizens Greening," presented at Reclaiming Vacant Properties: Building Leadership to Restore Communities conference (Louisville, Kentucky, June 3, 2009).

10. Vicki Been and Ioan Voicu, "The Effect of Community Gardens on Neighboring Property Values," *New York University Law and Economics Working Papers*, New York University School of Law, 2006.

11. John Kifner, "Giuliani's Hunt for Red Menaces," *New York Times*, December 20, 1999.

12. Paul Bairly, interview with the author, April 2, 2009.

13. Mike Hamm, "Best Practices: Linking Healthy Diets, Food Access, Neighborhoods, and Vacant Properties," presented at Reclaiming Vacant Properties: Building Leadership to Restore Communities conference (Louisville, Kentucky, June 2, 2009).

14. Joan Nassauer, interview with the author, March 4, 2009.

15. Rebecca Salminen Witt, interview with the author, December 2008.

16. Nassauer interview, March 4, 2009.

17. Rob Ruhlig, undated interview with the author.

18. Boyle interview, December 15, 2009.

19. John Gallagher, "Farming Detroit" and "Farm Could Make Detroit Hot Spot for Fresh Foods," *Detroit Free Press*, April 2, 2009.

20. Bill McGraw, "Farming Takes Root in Detroit: Hopes Spreads Along with the Compost," *Detroit Free Press*, May 4, 2009.

21. Witt interview, December 2008.

22. Kami Pothukuchi, interview with the author, December 11, 2009.

23. Matt Allen, author interview, March 23, 2009.

24. John Gallagher, "Detroit Council Is Split on Use of Riverfront Land: Watson's Idea of Using Leases Sparks Criticism," *Detroit Free Press*, July 18, 2005.

25. Ashley Atkinson, "Fostering Citizens Greening," presented at Reclaiming Vacant Properties (see note 9).

26. Majora Carter, interview with the author, December 2009.

27. Bill McKibben, *Deep Economy*, 63 (see note 5).

28. The quotes from Hamm in this section come from "Best Practices: Linking Healthy Diets, Food Access, Neighborhoods, and Vacant Properties," presented at Reclaiming Vacant Properties (see note 13).

29. "View Latest Craft Brewing Stats," *Brewers Association: A Passionate Voice for Craft Brewers*, Brewers Association, 2010, www.brewersassociation.org.

30. Susan Schmidt, interview with the author, December 17, 2009.

Chapter 4

1. Ian Lockwood, interview with the author, April 28, 2009.

2. John Gallagher, "Paths to Success: Movement Aims to Make Detroit an Easier City to Walk and Bike," *Detroit Free Press*, November 20, 2008.

3. A lawsuit by local attorney Richard Bernstein to force the commission to install on-demand crossing signals for blind and disabled people delayed the installation of the roundabouts but hasn't stopped it.

4. Tom Vanderbilt, *Traffic: Why We Drive the Way We Do (and What It Says About Us)* (New York: Knopf), 204–10.

5. Ibid, 210.

Chapter 5

1. Joan Nassauer's story of the shopping center that became Phalen Wetland Park is based on an author interview with her on March 4, 2009. See also Jennifer Dowdell, Harrison Fraker, and Joan Nassauer, *Replacing a Shopping Center with an Ecological Neighborhood*, available at www-personal.umich. edu/~nassauer/.../Vacant-property-now-tomorrow_Secure.pdf.

2. The story of the Cheonggyecheon follows the history outlined on the project's official website, www.metro.seoul.kr/kor2000/chungaehome/en/seoul/main.htm. See also Andrew C. Revkin, "Peeling Back Pavement to Expose Watery Havens," *New York Times*, July 16, 2009.

3. For more on the story of the Quaggy, see "Quaggy Waterways Action Group," at www.qwag.org.uk/home/ and *Case Study: River Quaggy Makes a Comeback*, Environment Agency, 2003–4, www.environment-agency.gov.uk/static/documents/Business/casestudyrecreation_1514776.pdf.

4. See *Case Study: River Quaggy Makes a Comeback* at www.grdp.org/static/documents/Business/casestudyrecreation_1514776.pdf. See also the case study *Quaggy River—Lewisham, London,* Commission for Architecture and the Built Environment, www.cabe.org.uk/case-studies/quaggy-river. See also *River Quaggy, Sutcliffe Park*, River Restoration Centre, 2008, www.therrc.co.uk/rrc_case_studies1.php?csid=46).

5. Ibid.

6. The Arcadia Creek story is based on 2009 site visits and an interview with David Feehan, former president of Downtown Kalamazoo Inc.

7. Richard Pinkham, *Daylighting: New Life for Buried Streams*, Rocky Mountain Institute, 2000, www.rmi.org/rmi/Library/W00-32_DaylightingNewLifeBuriedStreams.

8. Fritz Conradin and Reinhard Buchli, "The Zurich Stream Daylighting Program," in *Handbook of Regenerative Landscape Design*, ed. Robert L. France (Boca Raton, FL: CRC Press, 2008), 47–59.

9. Clarence M. Burton, *The City of Detroit Michigan 1701–1922,* vol. 1 (S. J.

Clarke, 1922), 83. The attempts to daylight Bloody Run and the story of the Adamah proposal are told in Steve Vogel, "Detroit (Re)Turns to Nature," in *Handbook of Regenerative Landscape Design*, 189–204.

10. The story of the piano was told to the author by architects involved in the restoration of the opera house in 1995. DiChiera succeeded, by the way, in creating his new opera venue there.

11. The Adamah vision says as much about Detroiters' distrust of outsiders as it does about daylighting itself. Just as America's nineteenth-century utopian communities like Brook Farm in Massachusetts rejected the more prosaic everyday world (at least for the short time until the community fell apart), Adamah envisions a self-directed community of Detroiters who have freed themselves from the shackles of a twenty-first-century economic system that seemingly has no place for them.

Chapter 6

1. The story of Liberty Lands Park is based on author interviews and a site visit on July 8, 2009. See also the website of the Northern Liberties Neighborhood Association, www.nlna.org.

2. Susan Wachter, *The Determinants of Neighborhood Transformations in Philadelphia—Identification and Analysis: The New Kensington Pilot Study*, The Warton School, University of Pennsylvania, 2004, http://gislab.wharton.upenn.edu/silus/Papers/GreeningStudy.pdf.

3. Paul Bairly, interview with the author, April 2, 2009.

4. Boyle interview (see chapter 2, note 1).

5. Kent State University's Cleveland Urban Design Collaborative, *Re-imagining Cleveland: Vacant Land Re-use Pattern Book*, April 2009, www.neighborhoodprogress.org/uploaded_pics/patternbookFINAL_lo-res_file_1241529170.pdf. Terry Schwarz, professor and head of Kent State University's Cleveland Urban Design Collaborative, led the Re-imagining Cleveland effort, with help from a Cleveland planning firm, McKnight Associates Ltd.

6. Interstate Technology & Regulatory Council Phytotechnologies Team, *Phytotechnology Technical and Regulatory Guidance and Decision Trees, Revised* (Washington DC: Interstate Technology & Regulatory Council, February

2009), www.itrcweb.org/guidancedocument.asp?TID=63. See also the United States Environmental Protection Agency's *Phytoremediation Resource Guide* (1999) available at www.cluin.org/download/remed/phytoresgude.pdf.

7. Kent State University's Cleveland Urban Design Collaborative, *Reimagining Cleveland* (see note 5).

8. Malcolm Gay, "Sculpture to Invigorate a Shrinking City," *New York Times*, July 5, 2009. See also the Citygarden website at www.citygardenstl.org.

9. Marilyn Wheaton, undated interview with the author.

10. This information comes from the Heidelberg Project's official website, www.heidelberg.org.

11. Dennis Alan Nawrocki, undated interview with the author. See also Dennis Alan Nawrocki, *Art in Detroit Public Places* (Detroit: Wayne State University Press, 2008).

12. The studies mentioned in the section can be found in James C. Schwab, ed., *Planning the Urban Forest: Ecology, Economy, and Community Development*, American Planning Association Planning Advisory Service Report Number 555 (Washington DC: American Planning Association, 2009).

13. Boyle interview (see chapter 2, note 1).

14. John Gallagher, "Leave It to Beaver to Prove River Cleaner; Animal Spotted in Detroit after 75-year Absence," *Detroit Free Press,* February 16, 2009.

15. Eric Sharp, "City Lots become Wildlife Habitats," *Detroit Free Press,* October 16, 2008.

16. Nassauer interview (see chapter 1, note 6).

Chapter 7

1. John Gallagher, "Nearly 3 in 10 in Detroit Need a Job," *Detroit Free Press*, August 28, 2009.

2. The estimate of at least fifty thousand foreclosures is taken from Diane McCloskey, director of communications, Detroit Office of Foreclosure Prevention & Response, author interview, September 2009. See also John Gallagher, "City's Fight Against Vacant Land Gets Tougher," *Detroit Free Press*, September 29, 2009.

3. Amber Arellano, "Stay the Course: Five Myths Drive Misguided Effort to Water Down Higher Standards of State's High School Curriculum," *Detroit News*,

September 10, 2009.

4. The information about TechTown and the quotes from Randal Charlton in this section are based on a site visit and an interview with Charlton on September 17, 2009. See also Charlton's blog entries at www.techtownwsu.org.

5. Chuck Robinson, interview with the author, September 16, 2009.

6. The information and quotes attributed to John Logue in this section come from an interview with the author, September 18, 2009.

7. The information and quotes attributed to Deborah Groban Olson in this section come from an interview with the author, September 11, 2009.

8. Castellani interview (see chapter 1, note 7).

9. The information here comes from the official website of the Mondragon Cooperative at www.mondragon-corporation.com.

10. The information about Evergreen Cooperatives comes from John Logue, author interview (see note 6). See also the Evergreen Cooperatives' website, www.evergreencoop.com. See also Gar Alperovitz, Ted Howard, and Steve Dubb, "Cleveland's Worker-Owned Boom," *Yes Magazine*, June 2009, www.yesmagazine.org/issues/the-new-economy/clevelands-worker-owned-boom.

11. Lindsay Chalmers, interview with the author, September 18, 2009.

12. Carla Javits quoted in "What does REDF do?" *REDF: Investing in Employment and Hope*, San Francisco: REDF, 2008, www.redf.org/about-redf.

13. Cheryl Dahle, "Balancing Act: The Right Size Scoop of Ice Cream," *Social Enterprise Reporter: Innovative Solutions for Social Entrepreneurs* November 2004: 1, 10–11 (www.google.com/url?sa=t&source=web&ct=res&cd=1&ved=0CAgQFjAA&url=http%3A%2F%2Fwww.sereporter.com%2Fpdf%2Fpremiere.df&rct=j&q=jim+schorr+scoop&ei=Z9erS7PkDIPIMob9rZkF&usg=AFQjCNGlU_xIFPqbOayNqhor0BGlAwc9GQ).

Chapter 8

1. Dan Kildee, interview with the author, February 20, 2009.

2. Frank Alexander, interview with the author, June 2, 2009.

3. Ibid. Land banks, however, don't need, and should not ask for government powers of eminent domain, Alexander said. Land banks should deal strictly with land that falls into their laps through tax foreclosure. If a city needs to take private land for a public use, then the city government itself should pursue that,

not the land bank.

4. Alexander interview (see note 2).

5. John Kromer, *Fixing Broken Cities: The Implementation of Urban Development Strategies* (New York: Routledge, 2010), 143.

6. Kildee interview, April 23, 2009.

7. Kildee interview, February 20, 2009.

8. Kildee interview, April 23, 2009.

9. Ibid.

10. The groups were the Local Initiatives Support Corporation (LISC), Community Development Advocates of Detroit, Community Legal Resources, and the Metropolitan Organizing Strategy Enabling Strength (MOSES).

11. Boyle interview (see chapter 2, note 1).

Chapter 9

1. John Gallagher, "Private Groups Push Detroit Ahead; Strapped City Hall Can't Do It All," *Detroit Free Press*, April 6, 2008.

2. Ibid.

3. Ibid.

4. Ibid.

Conclusion

1. Castellani interview (see chapter 1, note 7).

INDEX